THE WORKBOOK OF
INTERCESSORY PRAYER

THE
WORKBOOK OF
INTERCESSORY
PRAYER

Maxie Dunnam

Photo credits (in order of appearance)—Kenneth Murray: Rick Smolan; Rick Smolan; Kenneth Murray; A. Pierce Bounds; Rohn Engh / Sunrise Photos; Jane Word.

Quotations from the *Revised Standard Version* of the Bible, copyrighted 1946, 1952, and © 1971 by the Division of Christian Education, National Council of the Churches of Christ in the United States of America, are used by permission. The initials RSV are used to identify *Revised Standard Version* quotations.

Quotations from *The New English Bible,* © The Delegates of the Oxford University Press and the Syndics of the Cambridge University Press 1961 and 1970, are reprinted by permission. The initials NEB are used to identify *New English Bible* quotations.

The initials KJV are used throughout this book to identify quotations from the King James Version of the Bible.

Quotations from *The New Testament in Modern English,* by J. B. Phillips, are reprinted with permission of the Macmillan Company. Copyright © 1958 by J. B. Phillips.

New Testament quotations from *Today's English Version* of the New Testament (TEV), copyright by American Bible Society 1966, © 1971, and © 1976, are used by permission.

Quotations designated "Goodspeed" are from *The Short Bible: An American Translation,* edited by Edgar J. Goodspeed and J. M. Powis Smith, copyright 1935 by the University of Chicago.

First Printing, January, 1979(20)
Second Printing, May, 1979(20)
Third Printing, July, 1981(10)
Fourth Printing, June, 1982(10)
Fifth Printing, January, 1984(10)

Library of Congress Catalog Card Number: 78-65617
ISBN 0-8358-0382-1

Contents

Introduction

A PERSONAL WORD

One of the tensions of my life may be a tension common to many of us—the wide gap between belief and practice. So, I pray,

> Dear Master, in whose life I see
> All that I would, but fail to be;
> Let Thy clear light for ever shine,
> To shame and guide this life of mine.
>
> Though what I dream and what I do
> In my weak days are always two,
> Help me, oppressed by things undone,
> O Thou, whose deeds and dreams were one!
>
> JOHN HUNTER

This is akin to another tension I feel—the wide gap between the expectations of others and what I really am. I am committed to a recovery of prayer and a relevant spirituality. I have written in this area (*The Workbook of Living Prayer* and *Homesick for a Future*) and this is the current focus of my ministry with The Upper Room.

Many have a vision of what a spiritually relevant person ought to look like and think like and talk like. The vision usually grows out of a rigid understanding of piety and a stereotype of what it means to be spiritual.

Confession is in order. I do not consider myself anywhere near spiritual maturity. I go through seasons of struggle in believing. Sometimes I become very self-condemning, feeling hypocritical because I realize that I have not appropriated, nor do I live in experience what I know in my mind and heart. I have not learned well what I seek to teach others. I go through seasons of *dryness* rather regularly and have to call on my memory of God's activity in my past to sustain me in faith in the present.

I am publishing this workbook on intercession with deep reservations. I'm driven by the Spirit to do it because of the need in my own life and the clamoring need of people everywhere. In doing this I risk making myself vulnerable to you who read, because I'm saying right off that in my life of intercession I have only just begun. The demands of intercessory prayer, the mystery that surrounds it, the looming questions, my lack of total commitment and lack of proficiency—all swirl in my heart and head to intimidate and frighten me. "I believe, help my unbelief!"

Intercession is neither simple nor easy. So we don't walk this path without question, doubt, and reticence. I have overcome my reservation about offering this workbook, not because I have walked the path all the way, but because I want to.

I have discovered that putting it down in this fashion makes me less tentative and invites others to share the journey and give me company.

I have been working on this book for a long time. Yet, as I begin the actual writing, I am in Lucerne, Switzerland. I have been in two separate conferences and am awaiting a third. It is too expensive to fly back to the United States, then return ten days from now.

I've been away from home two weeks and have two more to go. I know no one in the city and I'm alone. Yesterday, my loneliness became devastating, so I did an extravagant thing. I called home. It was seven A.M. in Nashville, Tennessee, one P.M. in Lucerne, and my son, Kevin, answered the phone.

"Daddy! Where are you?"

"Lucerne, Switzerland."

"You sound as though you are across the street."

I talked to my wife and other two children. Afterward, I reflected upon the miracle that we were five thousand miles apart, an ocean separating us, yet, we talked personally, joyfully, intimately, and we heard clearly. I don't understand that. Oh, I studied about it in school, and with a little review, I could give you a layperson's explanation of how sound waves are carried by wire beneath the ocean and across the land from Lucerne to Nashville. But still I don't really understand it. It is beyond my comprehension.

Despite not understanding, I had no hesitation picking up the receiver, getting the overseas operator (I don't know where she was), and telling her to dial Nashville, Tennessee. I *knew* I could talk to my family across those thousands of miles of ocean and land. *So I did.* Likewise, I pray without much understanding.

Still, I am hesitant to write on intercessory prayer. I know very little about it and know no one who knows more than a very little about it. I don't understand it either. And yet, we can't think very long about prayer without thinking about intercessory prayer. We can't pray very long or very often without our minds and hearts turning from our own needs and our own relationship with God to others and their needs. Whether self-consciously or intentionally, when we are at prayer we speak the name of another, or in our thoughts we name others before God. Some of us may never have raised the question: What difference does it make? Or, does it make any difference? If it does, how does it make a difference? We continue to intercede even if we have never worked these questions through in our minds.

But there are many people who have given up prayer altogether because they do not understand or they have not seen that prayer makes a difference. Many who continue to pray have a great question mark about intercessory prayer. Therefore, even though they may be driven to name others in prayer—to call upon God to bless others in special ways—they have grave reservations about the validity and effectiveness of it.

Experiences in my own life have convinced me that *I don't have to understand intercessory prayer to practice it,* just as I don't have to understand the telephone to use it. It is hoped that this workbook will help us get on effectively and excitedly with that which we may never understand, but which is obviously a big part of God's plan for all of us.

I share as a groaning pilgrim with you; therefore, I urge you—as I counsel myself—*be patient with yourself and your spiritual growth.* Don't put out too many fleeces to prove God's action (see Judges 6:36-40). Don't be too intent on "results" you can easily measure. The realm of the Spirit is charged with mystery. God knows what kind of affirmation you need to keep you going. God will provide that. You simply need to be sensitive to it. Also, the meaning and purpose of it all is in our own growth and development, our own faithful obedience, our communion with God.

I would also prod you to a *life of gratitude.* God is doing far more than we normally recognize. Open your eyes, mind, and heart and see—see what God is doing. And when you don't see, or when you don't understand what you see, be grateful still. "In everything by prayer and supplication with thanksgiving" the power of Christ will come to you, however imperceptible in the beginning, until your eyes and heart and mind come alive to see all that he is doing in you and through you.

THE DESIGN

A WORKBOOK

This is a workbook. I present it in this fashion for two primary reasons. First, we learn to pray by praying. We never learn to pray by reading *about* prayer without also praying. This is not a book just to read, but one to participate in. This is called *experiential* learning. If you will respond to this style, bringing yourself and the content of your life to the content and guidance provided here, you will become *involved* in prayer. You will be praying.

Secondly, since I don't know much about prayer, especially intercessory prayer, it would be presumptuous of me to write a book, in the usual fashion of writing—as though I had something to say that had not already been said. What I want to provide is a workbook, a plan and guide for you to become *involved* in intercessory prayer. Many persons have helped to provide the content. Even when I am not quoting others directly, I will be sharing what I have learned from others—maybe saying in my own words what others have said better. The important dynamic will be your personal involvement in the content, your experiencing for yourself what you are reading about.

My previous *Workbook of Living Prayer* is meeting a lot of needs. At the time of this writing more than 150,000 are in print. I have been humbled and blessed by the response of hundreds of people who have taken the time to write or to speak to me personally about how their praying has been made meaningful and effective by the use of that workbook and, as a result, how their lives have been transformed. Believing that the secret of that book's effectiveness is in its practical and elementary style which calls for involvement, I offer *The Workbook of Intercessory Prayer* in similar format.

This workbook is to be seen neither as an argument for nor a defense of intercessory prayer. I am assuming that the reader already has some degree of commitment to intercession. Even so, questions and problems of intercession will be dealt with here. The focus of Week Three is upon *hurdles* we have to overcome. We will approach these hurdles, however, only after we have *immersed* ourselves in scripture. I believe that we will always have questions. These questions may at times be barriers to our praying. More often than not, though, we can live with the questions and still pray committedly and meaningfully if we keep in mind the witness of scripture and tradition and if we call upon our memory of God's working in our personal experiences.

THE PLAN

Here is the plan. This is a seven-week adventure. It is an individual journey, but my hope is that you will share it with some fellow-pilgrims who will meet together once each week during the seven weeks of the study. You are asked to give twenty to thirty minutes each day to work at making prayer a living experience, as your attention is guided to intercession. For most persons this twenty to thirty minutes will come at the beginning of the day. However, if it is not possible for you to give the time at the beginning of your day, do it whenever the time is available—but do it regularly.

The workbook is arranged in seven major divisions, each designed to guide you for one week. These divisions contain seven sections, one for each day of the week. Each day of the week will have three major aspects.

READING ABOUT PRAYER

In each day's section you will read something about prayer, not too much, but enough to provide something of the nature, meaning, and possibilities of prayer. Included in this will be some portions of scripture. The scripture is a basic resource for Christian living and praying.

REFLECTING AND RECORDING

Then each day, there will be a time for "reflecting and recording." This dimension calls you to record some of your reflections. The degree of meaning you receive from this workbook is largely dependent upon your faithfulness to its practice. You may be unable on a particular day to do precisely what is requested. If so, then simply record the fact and make a note why you can't follow through. This may give you insight about yourself and help you to grow.

Also, on some days there may be more suggestions than you can deal with in the time you have. Do what is most meaningful to you, and *don't feel guilty.*

The emphasis is upon growth, not perfection. Don't feel guilty if you do not follow exactly the pattern of the days. Follow the content and direction seriously, but not slavishly. Always remember that this is a personal pilgrimage. What you write is your private property. You do not have to share it with anyone. The importance of it is not what it may mean to someone else, but what it means to you. Writing, even if it is only brief notes or single-word reminders, helps us clarify our feelings and thinking. Such clarity is essential for prayer. (This means that every person must have a workbook. No two persons can share the same text.)

The significance of the reflecting and recording dimensions will grow as you move along. Even beyond the seven-week period, you will find meaning in looking back to what you wrote on a particular day in response to a particular situation.

DURING THE DAY

The third major aspect of the daily presentations is the "during the day" instructions. Here you are given suggestions for making your prayer experience a part of your whole life. The dynamic of prayer is communion with God. The goal of prayer is a life of friendship and fellowship with him, cooperating with his spirit, living his will in the world. So, you are asked to be intentional about moving from your specific time of prayer into a life of prayer by consciously seeking to relate all of life to God.

SHARING WITH OTHERS

In the history of Christian piety, the spiritual director or guide has been a significant person. To varying degrees, most of us have had spiritual directors—persons to whom we have turned for support and direction in our spiritual pilgrimage. There is a sense in which this workbook can be a "spiritual guide," for you can use it as a private venture without participating in a group.

Its meaning will be enhanced, however, if you share the adventure with eight to twelve others. In this way, the "priesthood of all believers" will come alive, and you will profit from the growing insights of others, and they will profit from yours. A guide for group sharing is included in the text at the end of each week.

If this is a group venture, all persons should begin their personal involvement with the workbook on the same day, so that when you come together to share as a group all will have been dealing with the same material and will be at the same place in the text. It will be helpful if you will have an initial get-acquainted group meeting to begin the adventure. A guide for this meeting is provided in this introduction.

Group sessions for this workbook are designed to last one and one-half hours (with the exception of this initial meeting). Those sharing in the group should covenant to attend all sessions unless an emergency prevents attendance. There will be seven weekly sessions following this first get-acquainted time.

A group consisting of eight to twelve members is about the right size. Larger numbers limit individual involvement.

One person can provide the leadership for the entire seven weeks, or leaders can be assigned from week to week. The leader's task is:

• to read directions and determine ahead of time how to handle the session. It may not be possible to use all the suggestions for sharing and praying together. Feel free to select those you think will be most meaningful and those for which you have adequate time. Be careful that you do not use all your time talking and not enough time for actual prayer;

• to model a style of openness, honesty, and warmth; (A leader should not ask others to share what he or she is not willing to share. Usually the leader should be the first to share, especially as it relates to personal experiences.)

• to moderate the discussion;

• to encourage reluctant members to participate, and try to prevent a few persons from doing all the talking;

• to keep the sharing centered in personal experience, rather than academic debate;

• to honor the time schedule; (If it appears necessary to go longer than one and one-half hours, the leader should get consensus for continuing another twenty or thirty minutes.)

• to see that meeting time and place are known by all, especially if meetings are held in different homes;

• to make sure necessary materials for meetings are available and that the meeting room is arranged ahead of time.

It is desirable that weekly meetings be held in the homes of the participants. (Hosts or hostesses should make sure there are as few interruptions as possible, e.g., children, telephone, pets, etc.) If meetings are held in a church, they should be in an informal, comfortable setting. Participants are asked to dress casually, to be comfortable and relaxed.

If refreshments are served, they should come after the meeting. In this way, those who wish to stay longer for informal discussion may do so, while those who need to keep to the one- and one-half-hour time schedule will be free to leave, but will get the full value of the meeting time.

SUGGESTIONS FOR INITIAL GET-ACQUAINTED MEETING

Since the initial meeting is for the purpose of getting acquainted and beginning the prayer pilgrimage, here is a way to get started. (If name tags are needed, provide them.)

1. Have each person in the group give his or her full name and the name by which each wishes to be called. Do away with titles. Address all persons by their first name or nickname. (Each person should make a list of the names somewhere in his/her workbook.)

2. Let each person in the group share one of the happiest, most exciting, or most meaningful experiences he/she has had during the past three or four weeks. After all persons have shared in this way, let the entire group sing the doxology ("Praise God, from Whom All Blessings Flow") or "Hallelu, Hallelu, Hallelu, Hallelujah, Praise Ye the Lord."

3. After this experience of happy sharing, ask each person who will to share his/her expectations of the pilgrimage. Why did he or she become a part of it? What does each expect to gain from it? What are the reservations?

4. The leader should now review the introduction to the workbook and ask if there are questions about directions and procedures (this means that the leader should have read the introduction prior to the meeting). If persons have not received copies of the workbook, the books should be handed out now. *Remember that every person must have his/her own workbook.*

5. Day One in the workbook is the day following this initial meeting, and the next meeting should be held on Day Seven of the First Week. If the group must choose another weekly meeting time other than seven days from this initial session, the reading assignment should be brought in harmony with that so that the weekly meetings are always on Day Seven, and Day One is always the day following a weekly meeting.

6. Since this is an experiment in intercession, ask that persons in the group pray by name for each other across the weeks to come as a part of the ongoing experience.

7. After checking to see that everyone knows the time and place of the next meeting, the leader may close with a prayer, thanking God for each person in the group, for the opportunity of growth, and for the possibility of learning to pray or of praying more meaningfully.

Getting Intercession
Into Perspective

DAY ONE
A Searching Question: What If?

I don't know when the question became so central in my thinking. It didn't emerge full blown. At first it was at the edge of my consciousness, but now it is at the center, pressing for attention. It's one of those "what if" questions that demands more action and life-response than it does reason or argument. "What if there are some things God either cannot or will not do until people pray?"

Even to ask the question may be shocking to some. It was to me when the Spirit first began to shape it in my mind. It is commonplace to think and affirm that God acts through persons. Deeds of mercy, acts of reconciliation, expressions of loving-kindness, deliberate righteous activity, performance that makes for peace—all are seen as God's work through persons. God's will is accomplished through us, we often say. On earth God's work must be our own.

Why is it such a long leap in our minds to think that God is as dependent upon our praying as he is upon our acting?

I have used the word *dependent* advisedly. I know it raises all sorts of theological red flags in many minds. To say that God is *dependent* upon us creatures for anything is probably presumptuous to say the least, and blasphemous, to say the most. Yet, I use the word deliberately and ask you to consider the question openly. *What if there are some things God either cannot or will not do until people pray?*

Stop for a minute or two and let the question burrow into your consciousness. Don't read any further until you have pondered the question.

REFLECTING AND RECORDING

Be honest and record in the space that follows what you think and feel about the question. Since we will reflect later on the question, register your honest response—in enough words to enable you to recall in the future what your initial response was.

Now read slowly the following story from Exodus 17:

> All the congregation of the people of Israel moved on from the wilderness of Sin by stages, according to the commandment of the Lord, and camped at Rephidim; but there was no water for the people to drink. Therefore the people found fault with Moses, and said, "Give us water to drink." And Moses said to them, "Why do you find fault with me? Why do you put the Lord to the proof?" But the people thirsted there for water, and the people murmured against Moses, and said, "Why did you bring us up out of Egypt, to kill us and our children and our cattle with thirst?"
>
> So Moses cried to the Lord, "What shall I do with this people? They are almost ready to stone me." And the Lord said to Moses, "Pass on before the people, taking with you some of the elders of Israel; and take in your hand the rod with which you struck the Nile, and go. Behold, I will stand before you there on the rock at Horeb; and you shall strike the rock, and water shall come out of it, that the people may drink." And Moses did so, in the sight of the elders of Israel. And he called the name of the place Massah and Meribah, because of the faultfinding of the children of Israel, and because they put the Lord to the proof by saying, "Is the Lord among us or not?"
>
> Then came Amalek and fought with Israel at Rephidim. And Moses said to Joshua, "Choose for us men, and go out, fight with Amalek; tomorrow I will stand on the top of the hill with the rod of God in my hand." So Joshua did as Moses told him, and fought with Amalek; and Moses, Aaron, and Hur went up to the top of the hill. Whenever Moses held up his hand [in prayer], Israel prevailed; and whenever he lowered his hand, Amalek prevailed.
>
> (Exodus 17:1-11, RSV)

Pray, now, however you wish, but make a commitment of yourself to be as faithful as possible in following through this experiment in prayer for seven weeks.

DURING THE DAY

Get the question firmly in your mind: *What if there are some things God either cannot or will not do until people pray?* Deliberately seek to recall that question and ponder it four or five times during the day.

DAY TWO
God's Promises Are Often Connected with Conditions to Be Met

The story of Israel's first battle which we read yesterday is marvelous in meaning. It is a dramatic story. The Israelites confronted the Amalekites in Rephidim. Joshua commanded the army of Israel; and Moses, Aaron, and Hur went up on the mountain to pray.

The fluctuations of the battle were astonishing. It was a see-saw of prevailing power. Israel would appear to be winning, then the Amalekites. The issue of the battle was soon discovered and the scripture states it clearly: "Whenever Moses held up his hand [in prayer], Israel prevailed; and whenever he lowered his hand, Amalek prevailed."

Not the fighters on the field of battle alone, but the intercessors on the mountain made the difference.

What if it is true—there are some things God cannot or will not do until people pray?

It is a mystery, yet scripture and Christian history offer some convincing evidence that God is as dependent upon our praying as he is upon our acting.

Even a cursory review of great biblical words confirms the fact that the promise of God to act in our lives and in history is often connected with a condition to be met. The classic Old Testament challenge and promise is an obvious example: "If my people who are called by my name humble themselves, and pray and seek my face, and turn from their wicked ways, then I will hear from heaven, and will forgive their sin and heal their land" (2 Chronicles 7:14, RSV).

The classic New Testament promise and challenge is from Jesus' allegory of the vine and the branches: "If you abide in me, and my words abide in you, ask whatever you will, and it shall be done for you" (John 15:7, RSV).

From history John R. Mott is a convincing witness. He testified:

> For years it has been my practice in traveling among the nations to make a study of the sources of spiritual movements which are doing most to revitalize and transform individuals and communities. At times it has been difficult to discover the hidden spring, but invariably where I have had the time and patience to do so, I have found it in an intercessory prayer life of great reality.

The big point here is that God's promises to act in our personal lives and in history are often connected with conditions which we must meet. This does not diminish the power and sovereignty of God. Nor does it make God capricious. It simply affirms the relationship that is ours with the Creator/Redeemer God. It underscores the fact that God has given us the superlative opportunity to be active participants in the fulfillment of his kingdom.

REFLECTING AND RECORDING

Take a brief survey of your religious pilgrimage. Can you locate some time when you began to think and feel that God was calling you to *action*—that you had to act out your faith, and that what you did would be a part of the accomplishment of God's will on earth. If you can locate such a time, record it here. Simply write enough to help you clarify and be specific.

Now, recall an action which you have performed in the past month which you really believe was something God wanted done, but that might not have been done had you not done it. Make a note of that action here.

Consider now the possibility that God is calling you to pray, even as he calls you to act. Reflect for a couple of minutes on that possibility, and write your thought here.

DURING THE DAY

There will be occasions today for you to *care for others,* to communicate God's love in your action. Don't miss those opportunities.

There will also be opportunities for you to *pray for others.* Be alert to those possibilities. Even though your prayer may be only a fleeting blessing, pray with the same deliberateness for persons you pass on the street or meet in the corridor or have conversation with on the phone.

DAY THREE
The Need for Millions of Praying People

> But we beseech you, brethren, to respect those who labor among you and are over you in the Lord and admonish you, and to esteem them very highly in love because of their work. Be at peace among yourselves. And we exhort you, brethren, admonish the idle, encourage the faint-hearted, help the weak, be patient with them all. See that none of you repays evil for evil, but always seek to do good to one another and to all. Rejoice always, pray constantly, give thanks in all circumstances; for this is the will of God in Christ Jesus for you.
>
> (1 Thessalonians 5:12-18, RSV)

A clergyperson heard Dr. Frank Laubach say, ''Prayer is the mightiest power on earth. *Enough* of us, if we prayed *enough,* could save the world—if we prayed *enough!*'' The clergyperson responded enthusiastically, ''If we could get Christians to stop and pray one minute a day, they could save the world.'' Dr. Laubach rebutted:

> I do not think that would be enough. The sun could keep nothing alive shining one minute a day. Life itself is dependent on the sun's rays, yet not one ray of light in a million produces life. Not one raindrop in a million finds its way to the roots of a tree. Not a seed in a million germinates. Not a shovelful of dirt in a million turns up a diamond in Kimberley. It is said that if all the eggs of the conger eel produced eels—and if they could find food—they would fill the space from here to the sun in two years. Nature is that extravagant! A very small proportion of our written or spoken words inspire men to *deeds.* So if we should find that our prayers do not always reach those for whom they are intended, but that every prayer probably reaches *somebody somewhere,* that is all we can ask, and more! Indeed, that fact is so powerful that if we of the Christian world pray persistently, and ''faint not,'' as Jesus commanded, we *shall* transform the world. But occasional feeble doubting prayers will get only feeble results. One minute a day will not save us![1]

Dr. Laubach was a man far ahead of his time in understanding the power of mind, thought, meditation, and prayer as a source of communicating to others. He knew that in our praying we do not persuade God to try harder or convince God as to the right answer for a particular problem. Rather it is other persons whom we persuade and convince. *Through our praying we assist God.*

When we pray for others, a mighty spiritual force lifts our minds and hearts toward God. His Spirit flows through our prayers to others, enabling God to speak to them directly. For this reason, Dr. Laubach sought to mobilize an army of ten million praying people, who would give themselves to an intentional ministry of prayer.

It would be a superficial game to talk about how many minutes of prayer per day would be required of ten million people to change the world. To even think that way misses Dr. Laubach's point and the exhortation of Paul to ''pray without ceasing.'' The need is for a continuous stream of spiritual power flowing from millions of praying people. This is the way Dr. Laubach put it.

Prayer is powerful, but it is not the power of a sledge hammer that crushes with one blow. It is the power of sun rays and rain drops which bless, because there are so many of them. Instead of a minute a day, we Christians must learn to flash *hundreds of instantaneous prayers* at people near and far, knowing that many prayers may show no visible results, but that at least some of them will hit their mark. When you fill a swamp with stones, a hundred loads may disappear under the water before a stone appears on the surface, but all of them *are necessary.*[2]

REFLECTING AND RECORDING

Look at the way you practice prayer. Record here your present style of praying:

How much time do you spend in prayer?

Where do you pray?

How do you pray?

You reflected yesterday upon the possibility that God may be calling you to pray even as he calls you to act. Now relate that to Dr. Laubach's challenge which you read today. Are there any changes you want to make in your prayer habits? Record them here.

DURING THE DAY

Dr. Laubach used to say, "Criticism of others nails them to the past. Prayer for them releases them into the future." Remember that in your relationships today.

DAY FOUR
The Same Old Question

I remember vividly an international theological consultation on inter-cessory prayer in which I participated in 1977. Thirty-one persons had come together at the invitation of the World Council of Churches. We represented a variety of prayer communities. All had special interest in prayer, and some had special theological expertise. Our practical task was to work out a prayer cycle of intercession for the churches of the world.

We had been together for two intensive days, hearing learned papers on prayer and discussing the theology of prayer and the place of intercession in the liturgy and life of the church. Because such diverse groups as Orthodox and Assemblies of God were represented, there was, unfortunately, an undercurrent of deep feelings about the nature of the church. What really *was* the church? The issue at stake was ecclesiastical ecumenism.

The hours were dragging, and a number of us felt we were skirting the issue and that too many people were on their own agenda. At a low point in the dialogue, an Anglican priest from England exploded, "What I want to know is, do we believe that anything happens as a result of our praying? If so, what?"

The tenor of the meeting changed, and for two hours there was a creative interchange involving not only the sharing of deep conviction and understanding of intercessory prayer, but also testimonies to the meaning and work of prayer in personal lives.

Here was the old question raised in a contemporary, somewhat sophisticated setting: Does God answer prayer?

It is precisely at this point—the granting of prayers—that even persons of deep faith and Christian commitment have difficulty. Sometimes this difficulty is enormous.

For a long period in my life—and occasionally even now—I was overly careful, even anxious about praying with the expectation of a specific response. It would be as though I were avoiding precise prayer to leave a way out in case the prayer were not granted.

Karl Barth has helped me here. This great theologian insisted that prayer, or praying, is simply asking. Prayer is permitted and commanded to us as petition. The Lord's Prayer is basically six petitions plus an address and doxology. Without question, Barth affirmed that our prayers are always answered, but he left room for discrepancy between the answer we receive and what we actually have asked. Barth was saying that God *cleanses* our prayers, using his wisdom in the answer we receive.

Still, this is the tug and tension in my life—a conflict between my confidence in God and the awareness that I have not received what I asked.

REFLECTING AND RECORDING

Spend a few minutes examining your own thoughts and feelings about whether God actually does answer prayer. Do you feel any of the tension or conflict I have confessed?

Check one of the following which most nearly reflects your conclusion:

( ) 1. When I was younger I didn't question it, but now I do.
( ) 2. I questioned it when younger, but do not question it now.
( ) 3. I have never thought about it.
( ) 4. I have thought a lot about it and still do.

How bold are you in being precise in your praying?

Very Bold _____ Bold _____ Timid _____ Vague _____

Now firmly fix this word of Jesus in your mind:

> Ask, and it will be given you; seek, and you will find; knock, and it will be opened
> to you. For every one who asks receives, and he who seeks finds, and to him who
> knocks it will be opened. Or what man of you, if his son asks him for bread, will
> give him a stone? Or if he asks for a fish, will give him a serpent? If you then, who
> are evil, know how to give good gifts to your children, how much more will your
> Father who is in heaven give good things to those who ask him!
> (Matthew 7:7-11, RSV)

Will you be willing to risk being bold and precise in your praying, especially when it is in another's behalf?

DURING THE DAY

On page 149 Matthew 7:7-11 is printed. Clip it and carry it in your pocket or purse for the next few days. Each time you see the paper, read it so that it will become a part of your memory.

DAY FIVE
Confidence/Ungranted Petitions

Yesterday we considered the common tension resulting from the conflict between our confidence in God and the awareness that we have not received specifically what we asked.

I am trying to be very precise in my language here. Note the emphasis of today; I am using the term *ungranted petitions*. This is different from what is generally termed *unanswered prayer*. Here we are centering on a struggle of faith.

I went through five or six years as a pastor unable to pray specifically for the healing of persons who were seriously ill. I would pray for "deliverance from too much pain," "strength to bear suffering," "guidance for doctors," or "support for loved ones." But not outright healing. I had prayed for the healing of too many who had died. This illustrates the lack of confidence that comes when our petitions are not granted.

This is what the pattern looks like. Becoming aware that I have not received that for which I asked, I begin to back away from praying for specific things. Question: Am I hedging in faith? Am I, in a way, limiting the lordship of Christ and giving in to a kind of skepticism?

Don't read any further until you spend two or three minutes pondering the problem and question from the perspective of your own experience.

Faith is not blind hope separated from reality. It does not affirm something that doesn't exist. Question: When I admit that my petitions have not been granted, am I abandoning faith? Wrestle with this question before you read on.

The New Testament is very explicit about precision in prayer. Along with the word of Jesus recalled yesterday, consider these. Don't rush through your reading of them.

> Therefore I tell you, whatever you ask in prayer, believe that you receive it, and you will.
>> (Mark 11:24, RSV)

> Hither to you have asked nothing in my name; ask, and you will receive, that your joy may be full.
>> (John 16:24, RSV)

> You did not choose me, but I chose you and appointed you that you should go and bear fruit and that your fruit should abide; so that whatever you ask the Father in my name, he may give it to you.
>> (John 15:16, RSV)

> Truly, truly, I say to you, he who believes in me will also do the works that I do; and greater works than these he will do, because I go to the Father.
>> (John 14:12, RSV)

So here is the dilemma: How do I continue to pray, believing that God answers when no answer seems evident? How do I continue to exercise faith in the face of ungranted petitions?

REFLECTING AND RECORDING

Write two or three sentences in the space that follows about how the above promises of Jesus presently affect your praying.

There are some great prayers that have come to us through the ages. Make your own the following prayer by Blaise Pascal from the seventeenth century:

> O Lord, let me not henceforth desire health or life, except to spend them for Thee, with Thee, and in Thee. Thou alone knowest what is good for me; do, therefore, what seemeth Thee best. Give to me, or take from me; conform my will to Thine; and grant that, with humble and perfect submission, and in holy confidence, I may receive the orders of Thine eternal Providence; and may equally adore all that comes to me from Thee; through Jesus Christ our Lord. Amen.

DURING THE DAY

Continue to work at implanting in your mind and heart the promise of Jesus you clipped from page 149 yesterday.

DAY SIX
Confidence and Faith

Yesterday we considered the conflict between confidence and ungranted petition. We raised the question whether admitting ungranted petitions was an abandonment of faith. If the answer to that is no, as I believe it is, then what happens to our confidence? What is the relation of confidence to faith?

Faith is not a confidence to be measured in human terms or by human limits. Faith refuses to quit praying, even when there seems to be evidence that we are not being heard. We push our confidence and hope beyond apparent defeat, and we continue to pray.

> He spoke to them in a parable to show that they should keep on praying and never lose heart: "There was once a judge who cared nothing for God or man, and in the same town there was a widow who constantly came before him demanding justice against her opponent. For a long time he refused; but in the end he said to himself, 'True, I care nothing for God or man; but this widow is so great a nuisance

that I will see her righted before she wears me out with her persistence.' " The Lord said, "You hear what the unjust judge says; and will not God vindicate his chosen, who cry out to him day and night, while he listens patiently to them? I tell you, he will vindicate them soon enough. But when the Son of Man comes, will he find faith on earth?"

(Luke 18:1-8, NEB)

Now here is a hard notion that causes us to grapple. In prayer—especially intercession—we often hope against hope—even to the point of arguing with God. Trembling in his presence, wrestling even with the thought of testing him, we continue to pray, renouncing what seems obvious (no answer) rather than accepting the thought that God is not able to reply.

Someone has made a very helpful distinction between *faith in prayer* and *prayer in faith. Faith in prayer* can be a perversion. Certainly *faith in prayer* may be presumptuous and clamorous, presenting ultimatums to God and demanding his acquiescence. But *prayer in faith* is different. It may ask and keep on asking. Indeed it may be clamorous. But all that the asking and pleading is, is entire submission to the will of God. Our faith is not in prayer, but in God. In prayer we may plead passionately for our needs, but our faith is in God; thus we can close our petitions as Jesus did, "Thy will be done."

Just recently I have been having excruciating pain in my shoulders and neck. This has gone on for four weeks. I have seen my doctor but have had no relief yet. The pain persists, often interrupting my sleep. I have prayed daily for ease. Three days ago I got an answer to my prayer, but no deliverance from my pain.

God's word to me was: Until you are relieved of your pain, use it as a call to prayer. Pray for the persons who will be coming to the retreat three weeks from now.

That hit me hard. I had covenanted with a small group to pray ardently for the retreat we were planning: for the persons who had already committed themselves to attend and for the persons we wanted to come who had not yet decided to do so. I had not faithfully kept that covenant.

God responded to my praying. I don't know when I'll be delivered from my pain, though I remain confident. In the meantime, I will keep my covenant to pray for the retreat.

Prayer in faith acknowledges God's sovereignty and rejoices in it. It is confident that all forces are ultimately under God's reign and power and that all things will work together for good for those who love God. Prayer, even persevering prayer, is a key to that working-together-for-good process.

REFLECTING AND RECORDING

Psalm 77 is the confession of a person who wrestled with the whole matter of confidence and faith, when thoughts of God issued only in a moan—and it seemed that God's love had ceased, that God's promises were at an end. Was God angry or had he forgotten? The psalmist then remembered the *movement* of God which was the context of faith. Not only did he look back on his own life but on God's activity in history. That kept faith alive. Ponder this psalm.

I cry aloud to God,
　　aloud to God, that he may hear me.
In the day of my trouble I seek the Lord;
　　in the night my hand is stretched
　　　　out without wearying;
　　my soul refuses to be comforted.

I think of God, and I moan;
　　I meditate, and my spirit faints.
Thou dost hold my eyelids from closing;
　　I am so troubled that I cannot speak.

I consider the days of old,
　　I remember the years long ago.
I commune with my heart in the night;
　　I meditate and search my spirit:
"Will the Lord spurn forever,
　　and never again be favorable?
Has his steadfast love for ever ceased?
　　Are his promises at an end for all time?
Has God forgotten to be gracious?
　　Has he in anger shut up his compassion?"
And I say, "It is my grief
　　that the right hand of the Most High has changed."

I will call to mind the deeds of the Lord;
　　yea, I will remember thy wonders of old.
I will meditate on all thy work,
　　and muse on thy mighty deeds.
Thy way, O God, is holy.
　　What god is great like our God?
Thou art the God who workest wonders,
　　who hast manifested thy might
　　　　among the peoples.
Thou didst with thy arm redeem thy people,
　　the sons of Jacob and Joseph.
When the waters saw thee, O God,
　　when the waters saw thee, they were afraid,
　　yea, the deep trembled.
The clouds poured out water;
　　the skies gave forth thunder;
　　thy arrows flashed on every side.
The crash of thy thunder was in the whirlwind;
　　thy lightnings lighted up the world;
　　the earth trembled and shook.
Thy way was through the sea,
　　thy path through the great waters;
　　yet thy footprints were unseen.
Thou didst lead thy people like a flock
　　by the hand of Moses and Aaron.
　　　　　　(Psalm 77, RSV)

Write your own prayer expressing your deepest feelings to God in regard to your confidence and faith. Note: Before you write your prayer, reflect upon the choices you checked on Day Four.

DURING THE DAY

Look at the day which is before you. What is the most difficult situation or relationship you will face? Record that situation or relation here.

Dedicate this situation or relationship to God. Determine now that as you face it you will remember and claim the promise that "all things work together for good to them that love God."

DAY SEVEN
When No Desire Is There

If I've heard it once, I've heard it a hundred times: "But what if I don't feel like praying? What if there is no desire, no sense of need, no pull to pray?"

For each person who has expressed such honesty, there are scores who have not been so open.

It happens to most of us. To some more frequently than others. Desire and the sense of need to pray are absent. This makes prayer difficult, some feel impossible. Sometimes this happens when we are disappointed in prayer. The "no-answer" or "no-response" we have received to our own petitions or intercessions lead us to doubt. Doubt conditions us for the devil to be more effective in our lives. Doubt *can* be very constructive, but this kind of doubt is more paralyzing than constructive.

If you were in that shape now, you probably wouldn't be using this workbook. Or, you may be in that condition now. But perhaps you can remember times when you did receive guidance and that memory gives you the intuition to do what I am about to counsel you to do.

One, *in penitence return to God.* We fall back on our commitment to our own relatedness to God. This is our first and supreme need when we are out of touch, when we don't feel like praying, when our sensitivity to the needs of others is so dull that we are not driven to prayer. A renewal of spirit, even a reconversion which only God can give, is the only answer.

On the way to realizing a renewal of spirit, even a reconversion, we can "say" prayers though we don't feel like praying. Even a once meaningful child's form of prayer which we have long since discarded is worth recalling and practicing.

Two, *continue or renew your worship customs,* especially those practices of corporate worship where the community of faith celebrates God's action in history. Holding to these outward practices, though the inner meaning of them may be gone, is an obedient response from you to God. It may be a bare homage, but it is a symbol that will keep the possibility of renewal real in your mind and heart.

A third thing that is helpful in these times of the absence of desire to pray or the sense of need is to *talk honestly about your feelings with caring friends*. Such honest sharing often brings perspective to your "dryness." Your friends can love and sustain you as you move through your valley.

REFLECTING AND RECORDING

If you presently feel that love for God and others seems dead or the desire to pray is gone and you are numb in sensing need, you know how difficult it is to decide what you need to do, and act upon it. If your prayer life is currently strong, you are in an ideal position to plan for those times now.

Formulate a firm resolve for deliberate action on your part and write your commitment here, so you can call upon it when you need it.

Mother Teresa of Calcutta has said, "Prayer enlarges the heart until it is capable of containing God's gift of himself." Pray now that your heart will grow to that size.

If you are sharing this prayer adventure with others, your weekly meeting should be some time today. Pray by name for those who will be coming that the sharing will be open and honest and that the group will truly become a *prayer* group.

DURING THE DAY

Remember to think about (anticipate) and pray for your group meeting throughout the day.

GROUP MEETING FOR WEEK ONE

INTRODUCTION

These group sessions will be meaningful to the degree that they reflect the experience of all the participants. The guide is simply an effort to facilitate personal sharing. Therefore, do not be rigid in following these suggestions. The leader, especially, should seek to be sensitive to what is going on in the lives of the participants and to focus the group sharing on those experiences.

Ideas are important. We should wrestle with new ideas as well as with ideas with which we disagree. It is important, however, that the group meeting not become a debate about ideas. The emphasis should be upon persons—experiences, feelings, and relationships.

The more the group comes to trust one another honestly and openly sharing what is happening in their lives, the more meaningful the experience will be. This does not mean sharing only the good, or positive; share also the struggles, the difficulties, the negatives. Building a life of prayer involves struggles and change. We may not always "feel" God's presence. Therefore praying is not dependent upon feeling. Don't be afraid to share your "dry periods," your valleys, your plateaus, as well as your mountains.

SHARING TOGETHER

1. Begin your session together by allowing time for each person in the group to share his/her most meaningful day with the workbook this week. The leader should begin this sharing. Tell why that particular day was so meaningful.

2. Now share your most difficult day. Tell what you experienced and why it was so difficult.

3. Ask all persons in the group to share their personal response to the problem of avoiding praying precise prayers, as related on Day Four—"to leave a way out in case my prayer is not granted." Some may have already done this in response to questions one and two above. Let others talk about their own reservation or failure about being precise in prayer and expecting answers.

4. Ask each person in the group to share one of the most meaningful prayer experiences of his/her life.

PRAYING TOGETHER

Background note: Suggestions for this "praying together" time will be given each week. The leader for the week should examine these ahead of time—regard them only as suggestions. What is happening in the meeting—the mood, the needs that are expressed, the timing—should determine the direction of the group's praying togetre is power in corporate prayer, and it is important that this dimension be included in our prayer pilgrimage. Corporate prayer is one of the great blessings of the Christian community. It is important, however, that each participant feels comfortable in this. No pressure will be placed on anyone to pray aloud. *Silent* corporate prayer is as vital and meaningful as verbal corporate prayer. The group should spend at least ten or fifteen minutes (usually at the close) of each group meeting in corporate prayer.

INTRODUCTION OF CLOSING PRAYER EXPERIENCE

God does not need to hear our verbal words to hear our prayers. Silence, where thinking is centered and attention is focused, may provide our deepest periods of prayer. There is power, however, in a community on a common journey verbalizing their thoughts and feelings to God in the presence of their fellow pilgrims.

Verbal prayers should be offered spontaneously as a person chooses to pray aloud—not, "Let's go around the circle now, and each one pray."

Gratitude is a primary dimension of prayer—private and corporate. Ask each person to think of one thing for which he or she is grateful. Hopefully some of these will be experiences from this sharing session, as well as from the personal prayer ventures of the week. Let each person name these aloud in a word or a sentence. As a person names something, the group responds: *Lord, we thank you.*

Let the group think back over the personal needs or concerns that came out of sharing this session. Within the group begin to speak these aloud with any person verbalizing a need or concern that has been expressed. Don't hesitate to mention a concern that you may have picked up from another, such as: "John expressed the fact that he is in a dry period in his spiritual life. Let's pray that he will be able to follow the suggestions made today until he experiences a renewal."

As concerns are verbalized, it will be helpful for each person to make notes of the concerns. There is space for this in the margins of your workbook. These can be referred to as continuing concerns for prayer in the coming week.

All of this will be in silence as each person prays in his/her own way. The leader ends with a verbal sentence prayer.

Let the leader close this time of prayer by saying something like, "One day this week we considered the possibilities that God calls us to pray as well as to act and that he may be as dependent upon our praying as upon our acting. May each one of us stay open to these possibilities. Let's be sure to pray for each other throughout the coming week. God bless you!"

After all concerns have been given, enter deliberately into a period of silence. Let the leader verbalize successively each of the needs that have been mentioned, allowing a brief period following each concern so that persons in the group may center their attention and focus their prayers on the person, need, or concern mentioned.

Immersing Ourselves In Scripture 2

DAY ONE
Prayer as Communion with God

We must not (nor shall we) move far into our consideration of prayer without getting clear one principle that is the umbrella under which all our praying takes place. *Prayer is communion with God.*

The primary focus of this workbook is *intercession. The Workbook of Living Prayer* published by The Upper Room is a more general experiment with prayer in which great emphasis is placed on prayer as communion with God. Though I can't repeat that total emphasis here, still we need to remind ourselves often that the great gift of God in prayer is himself. Whatever else God gives, however great and significant, is incidental and secondary to God's gift of relationship.

Here is an expression of prayer as communion. Read it slowly.

O God, thou art my God, I seek thee,
  my soul thirsts for thee;
my flesh faints for thee
  as in a dry and weary land where
    no water is.
So I have looked upon thee in the
  sanctuary,
  beholding thy power and glory.
Because thy steadfast love is better
    than life,
  my lips will praise thee.
My soul is feasted as with marrow
    and fat,
  and my mouth praises thee with
    joyful lips,
when I think of thee upon my bed,
  and meditate on thee in the
    watches of the night.
      (Psalm 63:1-3,5-6, RSV)

Keeping this perspective of prayer as communion with God saves us from some common pitfalls. One is our temptation to reduce prayer only to

petitions and to seek to cultivate techniques that will assure effectiveness in getting what we want. Another pitfall is a private exercise in self-communion in which we practice *auto-suggestion,* soothing our own anxieties and purifying our own thought.

There is nothing wrong with petition. Asking implies that another is with you and that you are communicating. Asking also means faith in some kind of response. This entire adventure is designed to give meaning and power to intercession, which is a form of petitionary prayer. And, there is nothing wrong with auto-suggestion *per se,* but auto-suggestion alone is not Christian prayer.

Christian prayer involves both petition and self-communion, but the heart of prayer is neither. The essential nature of prayer is in communion with God. In that communion, what is false in petition is cleansed. Self-communion and auto-suggestion are transcended, and all that is true is emphasized. Harry Emerson Fosdick has distilled the essence of Jesus' prayer life to make clear that the central meaning of prayer is communion with God.

> To Jesus, . . . the meaning of prayer was not that God would give him whatever he asked. God did not. That sustained and passionate petition where the Master thrice returned with bloodstained face, to cry, "Let this cup pass" (Matt. 26:39), had "No" for an answer. Neither did prayer mean to Jesus merely the reflex action of his own mind. Jesus prayed with such power that the one thing which his disciples asked him to teach them was how to pray (Luke 11:1); he prayed with such conscious joy that at times the very fashion of his countenance was changed with the glory of it (Luke 9:28, 29). Can you imagine him upon his knees then *talking to himself?* Was he merely catching the rebound of his own words? *Surely, when the Master prayed, he met somebody.* His life was impinged on by another Life. He felt "a Presence that disturbed him with the joy of elevated thoughts." His prayer was not monologue, but dialogue; not soliloquy, but friendship. *For prayer is neither chiefly begging for things, nor is it merely self-communion; it is that loftiest experience within the reach of any soul, communion with God.*[3]

REFLECTING AND RECORDING

Write a brief prayer, four or five sentences, which is an expression of your experience of or longing for communion with God. You may want to read again the above psalm.

DURING THE DAY

God is present with us always. Prayer is *consciousness* of his presence; consciousness can lead to communion with him. Acknowledge God's presence throughout the next twenty-four hours, but decide now that at certain times you will channel your consciousness to the deeper level of *communion* with him.

As you anticipate your day, list two or three times when you will strive to give yourself to a consciousness of God's presence:

DAY TWO
God Loves Me

Were you able to follow through with the specific times you set aside yesterday for deliberate consciousness and communion with God?

If not, why not?

If so, did that awareness move deeper into communion?

Did it make any difference?

Spend a bit of time reflecting in response to these questions before you move on.

The more intentional and disciplined I become in my prayer life, the more obvious it becomes that I must immerse myself in scripture. The Bible is our primary prayer source book.

Though scripture will be a significant part of our daily attention for this entire adventure in intercessory prayer, during this second week we will immerse ourselves in scripture in a special way. The goal is to *hear* and *experience* the word of God in order to move with faith and conviction into a life of intercession.

Yesterday we gained perspective by considering communion with God as the essence of prayer. Today reflect upon what, on the surface, may appear obvious: GOD REALLY LOVES ME.

Don't dismiss this statement too quickly. Deep in the heart of many of us there is the lurking feeling that all the things we hear about God's love for us are not really true.

How often in my counseling do I try to reassure persons in their depression that God really loves them? They will nod a positive assent without accepting the powerful reality of the fact of God's love. I can understand such verbal assent without actual acceptance because I've been there, too—often. It is easy to affirm God's love if we keep it general. God loves *us*. But the crucial issue is in the statement: "God loves me." That is where the lurking feelings of doubt emerge.

Two weeks after I became World Editor of *The Upper Room* (a monumental task for which I felt incapable, yet to which I felt a definite call) I had an automobile accident. The pain and incapacity that came from a broken leg, broken ribs, and punctured lung, added to my feelings of inadequacy about my new job combined to bring depression and anxiety. I was unable to find meaning in the events, and my mood often verged on bitterness.

During that time I spent hours with scripture and discovered the witness is clear. God loves us! One day, during that period, one of the most powerful statements of God's love in the entire Bible became a personal word from God to me.

> But now thus says the Lord, he who created you, O Jacob, he who formed you,
>   O Israel:
> "Fear not, for I have redeemed you; I have called you by name, you are mine.
> When you pass through the waters I will be with you;
>   and through the rivers, they shall not overwhelm you;
> when you walk through fire you shall not be burned, and the flame shall not
>   consume you.
> For I am the Lord your God,
>   the Holy One of Israel, your Savior.
>   (Isaiah 43:1-3*a*, RSV)

I received that word as a personal affirmation, confirming God's love of me. I look back upon the weeks following that accident as one of the most significant growth periods of my life.

REFLECTING AND RECORDING

Spend two or three minutes reflecting upon whether you can say with conviction, "God loves *me*."

Locate in your memory some specific experiences or occasions when you knew you were loved by God. Record one of those experiences here.

Put here the names of two or three persons whom you feel need to know that they are loved by God.

_____

_____

_____

Note: Do not proceed until these persons have been named, because you will be praying for them all this week.

Pray now that you will become more conscious of the love of God in your life, and the conviction that he really loves you will become deeper. Then pray by name for the persons you have listed.

DURING THE DAY

On page 149, the scripture from Isaiah is printed with blank spaces at certain points. Write your name in those blanks, clip out the passage, and carry it with you for the remainder of this week. Take it out now and then and read it. Hopefully you will have committed it to memory before the week is past.

DAY THREE
God Loves Me

I don't know why it is, but in my own experience I know that it is not enough to be touched just once by the love of God. It takes more—much more—and often it takes a long time and persistent effort to believe that I am loved by God as I am.

Memory helps here. Yesterday you recalled some experiences of awareness of God's love. Take two or three minutes now to get in touch again with those experiences or to try to remember other times when you were sure God loved you.

Ponder now some other great affirmations of God's love from scripture.

> For the mountains may depart
>   and the hills be removed,
> but my steadfast love shall not depart from you,
>   and my covenant of peace shall not be removed,
>   says the Lord, who has compassion on you.
> (Isaiah 54:10, RSV)

> Can a woman forget her sucking child,
>   that she should have no compassion
>   on the son of her womb?
> Even these may forget,
>   yet I will not forget you.
> Behold, I have graven you on the
>   palms of my hands. . . .
> (Isaiah 49:15-16, RSV)

The Lord is merciful and gracious,
   slow to anger and abounding in
      steadfast love.
He will not always chide,
   nor will he keep his anger for ever.
He does not deal with us according
      to our sins,
   nor requite us according to our iniquities.
For as the heavens are high above the earth,
   so great is his steadfast love toward
      those who fear him;
as far as the east is from the west,
   so far does he remove our transgressions
      from us.
As a father pities his children,
   so the Lord pities those who fear him.
For he knows our frame;
   he remembers that we are dust.
         (Psalm 103:8-14, RSV)

The ultimate effort of God to convey his love to us is in Jesus Christ. The entire New Testament witnesses to that. The suffering and death of Jesus for us—the fulfillment of his word, "Greater love has no man than this, that a man lay down his life for his friends" (John 15:13, RSV)—is that love at its pinnacle.

Jesus *lived* and *died* his love for us. He also used the simplest human images to give flesh to his love. He chose, for example, the image of a shepherd, so familiar to his hearers. They knew the devotion of a shepherd for his sheep. So, Jesus dared to say, "I am the good shepherd. I know my sheep and my sheep know me . . . and I am giving my life for my sheep" (John 10:14-15, Goodspeed). In another place the image is made even more explicit: "If one of you has a hundred sheep and loses one of them, does he not leave the ninety-nine in the open pasture and go after the missing one until he has found it? How delighted he is then! He lifts it on to his shoulders, and home he goes to call his friends and neighbours together. 'Rejoice with me!' he cries, 'I have found my lost sheep' " (Luke 15:4-6, NEB).

Then he adds a specific application so that his hearers will not lose themselves in the simplicity of the image: "In the same way, I tell you, there will be greater joy in heaven over one sinner who repents than over ninety-nine righteous people who do not need to repent" (Luke 15:7, NEB).

When I immerse myself in scripture, I know GOD LOVES ME.

REFLECTING AND RECORDING

The love of God also comes to us through other persons. In the experiences of God's love you recalled yesterday, did your awareness of God's love come through another person?

Name the person _____

Recall a separate experience when you were forgiven, accepted, helped; when you were given to when you didn't deserve it. Write enough about that experience, a sentence or two or a few key words, that will establish it in your mind.

Was this the love of God given through a person? Thank God for this person and others who have shared his love.

Intercession may be seen as the act of remembering another before God. We intentionally hold another person before God in conscious thought, imagination, and memory. With that understanding, now pray for the persons you named yesterday as needing an awareness of God's love.

DURING THE DAY

Seek to be sensitive to the ways God will communicate his love to you today, and how he wants to communicate his love to another through you. Continue to carry Isaiah 43:1-3 with you and consider it as often as possible.

DAY FOUR
My God Will Hear Me

The power of prayer rests in the faith that God who loves us hears us.

Some months ago my wife, Jerry, came upon an article in *The Inquirer* about ten-year-old Kay Sidle. She was attracted to the article because the picture of little Kay looked amazingly like our middle daughter Kerry. The banner headline proclaimed, "Brave little girl, who has only months to live, needs your cheerful letters." The article said, "Quiet, gentle little Kay is dying. A brain tumor the size of a golf ball is killing her."

The tumor had been removed by surgery once, but had regrown, and the doctors felt that another surgery would be futile and would only hasten death. Sometimes it takes six shots a day to make the pain bearable for Kay. The mother of Kay was requesting cheerful letters to prevent Kay from being so lonely.

There is something in that request alone that bears a lot of consideration —a mother pleading through a newspaper for letters to assuage the loneliness of her dying daughter—but that's another dimension than the one I want to share here.

When this article appeared, my wife and I were participating in a prayer group with five other couples. This became a crucial matter at our house. It became a matter of anguish and search and trauma—even a crisis in faith. Little Kay became a part of Jerry's life. Though over a thousand miles away, Kay was a part of our household in Nashville.

Jerry went through all sorts of faith contortions—praying for Kay—but not really knowing how to pray for her. "Would God heal her?" If God would not heal her, why would he let her live? Why? What did God have to do with this? If he had anything to do with it, what kind of God was he? These were not sophomoric questions to tickle intellectual fancy. Jerry was involved with little Kay and she was involved with God. Because of her praying she could no longer be independent either of God or of Kay.

I will never forget the morning when Jerry—her face wet with tears—came from her time of prayer with this word: "I don't understand it—I will never understand it— I don't know what God is doing, or what he can do—but I know that he is at least doing exactly what I am doing—hurting and crying for little Kay."

What a breakthrough! What an experience of God in prayer!

It is at the heart of prayer to know that God loves us and that we are *heard* by Divine Love. The scripture affirms it over and over.

> Therefore the Lord waits to be
> gracious to you;
> therefore he exalts himself to
> show mercy to you.
> For the Lord is a God of justice;
> blessed are all those who wait for him.

Yea, O people in Zion who dwell at Jerusalem; you shall weep no more. He will surely be gracious to you at the sound of your cry; when he hears it, he will answer you.

(Isaiah 30:18-19, RSV)

But know that the Lord has set apart the godly for himself; the Lord hears when I call to him.

(Psalm 4:3, RSV)

O thou who hearest prayer! To thee shall all flesh come.
(Psalm 65:5, RSV)

I call upon thee, for thou wilt answer me, O God; incline thy ear to me, hear my words.

(Psalm 17:6, RSV)

But as for me, I will look to the Lord, I will wait for the God of my salvation; my God will hear me.

(Micah 7:7, RSV)

Ask, and it will be given you; seek, and you will find; knock, and it will be opened to you. For every one who asks receives, and he who seeks finds, and to him who knocks it will be opened.

(Matthew 7:7-8, RSV)

Without the faith that God loves us and hears us, it is not likely that we will pray very much. The confidence that God hears our prayers rings throughout scripture. The above scriptural affirmations, climaxed by the promise of Jesus—whoever asks, receives, whoever seeks finds, and for the one who knocks the door is opened—are clear calls to confident prayer.

I am dependent upon Andrew Murray for impacting my life so forcefully with this simple but powerfully profound truth—"My God will hear me." In a moving chapter in his book, *The Ministry of Intercession,* I was first called to ponder the immense meaning of God as a "prayer-hearing God."

Perhaps you have felt no need to consider that. You may have accepted that God hears your prayers. That is not my case, however. I have struggled with whether my prayers were being heard by God. I believe this to be a crucial matter.

Murray is right. "The power of prayer rests in the faith that God hears it. In more than one sense this is true. It is this faith that gives a man courage to pray. It is this faith that gives him power to prevail with God. The moment I am assured that God hears *me* too, I feel drawn to pray and to persevere in prayer. I feel strong to claim and to take in faith the answer God gives. One great reason for lack of prayer is the want [lack] of the living, joyous assurance: My God will hear me." [4]

REFLECTING AND RECORDING

If you were totally confident that God would hear you, exactly what would you say to him now? Write your words here.

Hold again before God in prayer the persons you feel need to experience divine love.

DURING THE DAY

"My God will hear me" is a strong affirmation. Get this affirmation vividly in your mind. "My God will hear me." See how many times you can repeat it to yourself during the next twenty-four hours.

DAY FIVE
My God Hears Me . . . and Answers

"My God hears me." During the past twenty-four hours did you consciously try to call this affirmation to mind? How many times did you repeat it to yourself? Making affirmations is an important principle of life—and especially of prayer. We live by affirmations. Maybe not consciously, but what we deeply believe affects how we live. Whether we believe God hears us will certainly determine our praying. It is important, then, to root it deeply in our minds and hearts, "My God hears me."

Turn back to yesterday and reread the scripture about God hearing.

This is an almost incomprehensible grace—to be heard by God. Weak creature, feeble as I am, my God hears me! Sinner though I be, often violating his will, God hears me! Undisciplined seeker, haphazard pray-er, God hears me!

Amazing grace! I am not left to myself and my own power. I am not dependent alone on my friends. "My God hears me!"

Not only does he hear, *he answers.*

> But thou, O Lord, art a shield about me,
>   my glory, and the lifter of my head.
> I cry aloud to the Lord,
>   and he answers me from his holy hill.
>   (Psalm 3:3-4, RSV)

On Day Four of Week One I referred to Karl Barth's insistence that our prayers are always answered. Barth insisted on this because his first criterion of prayer is based upon our freedom before God. God has given us permission to pray, and because this permission is given by God, it becomes a command, even a necessity. *God wills that we should pray.* Even so, prayer is grace, an offer of God. It is unthinkable that God would will us to do something that would not make a difference. In the will of God that we should pray is the assurance that *God hears what God commands, and what God hears God answers.* Our prayers become a part of God's plan and will.

Father John Powell helped me get a handle on how God answers us. God speaks through my *mind,* giving me new ideas and new perspectives. God speaks through my *will,* giving me new desires or rekindling desires that have lost vitality, thus infusing me with power. God speaks through my *emotions,* comforting me, calming me, troubling me, stirring me up, making me restless, healing me or giving me peace. God speaks through my *imagination,* speaking to me, internally, words I need to hear. God speaks through my *memory.* When I need it, God stirs a stored up memory to remind me of something in the past which is relevant to my need in the present—an experience, a word, a relationship in which I was with God and I heard, felt, and knew God.

So prayer is a two-way, not a one-way process. We speak, God hears.

God speaks, we hear. Sometimes God's *answering* may involve confirming our expectations, thwarting our trust in ourselves, or opening an unexpected door. Amazing grace! My God hears me—and answers!

REFLECTING AND RECORDING

Recall and record here your most recent experience of speaking to God when you were confident that he heard. Describe the experience enough to get it clearly in mind.

Were you aware of a specific answer from God? Record that also.

Pray for the three persons you named who need an awareness of God's love.

DURING THE DAY

Add to your affirmation and call it to mind as often as possible today. Your new affirmation: "My God hears me—and answers." This affirmation is printed twice on page 149. Cut these out and put them in two frequently seen places, e.g., your bathroom mirror or the refrigerator door.

DAY SIX
Ask, Seek, Knock

We don't want to leave without certainty this matter of God's hearing and answering. *The assurance that we will be heard and answered is the chief lesson scripture teaches about prayer.* Jesus states this twice in the Sermon on the Mount.

In Matthew 6:6 he says, "But when you pray, go into your room and shut the door and pray to your Father who is in secret; and your Father who sees in secret will reward you" (RSV). He comes back to it in Matthew 7:7-8, "Ask, and it will be given to you; seek, and you will find; knock, and it will be opened to you. For every one who asks receives, and he who seeks finds, and to him who knocks it will be opened" (RSV).

In this second passage he distinctly states the promise twice. He obviously is intent on impressing us with the fact that we *may* and *must* confidently expect an answer to our prayer. Next to the revelation of the Father's love for each of us, there is no more important lesson in the school of prayer than this:

"EVERY ONE WHO ASKS RECEIVES."

The fact that the Lord reiterates this lesson shows that he knows our hearts. Our doubt and distrust are altogether too natural for our own good. So, we casually practice prayer as a religious exercise, without expectation of an answer. Believing prayer, with the expectation of an answer, is often too much work and requires too much faith for half-hearted disciples.

Here may be the most shocking truth for most of us:

IF WE ASK AND RECEIVE NOT, IT MAY BE BECAUSE SOMETHING IS AMISS OR LACKING IN OUR PRAYING.

The apostle James sounded that truth. "Ye ask, and receive not, because ye ask amiss" (James 4:3, KJV).

The great lesson from Jesus, confirmed by this word from James is that if there is no apparent answer to our prayer, the problem is not solved by giving up. Nor should we always assume that something is wrong with our faith. There are other reasons than ill-formed or ill-motivated praying for unanswered prayer. We are not to lose confidence. We seek to let the word and Spirit teach us to pray aright.

That is added reason for immersing ourselves in scripture—that the word will explain itself to us as we believe and that the Spirit will teach us to pray. We are not, then, to submit to our weak faith and settle for *no answer*. Rather, we are to yield ourselves to be searched, even purified, by the Spirit, until our prayer is the confident prayer of faith which expects and receives an answer. Martin Luther said one cannot "pray uncertainly." "Amen" is explained in the Heidelberg Catechism to mean "this shall be true and certain."

I mentioned in the introduction that I began writing this workbook while in

Geneva. As I returned from that trip my luggage was lost in New York. For days I struggled in prayer over that matter. For some reason I could not pray specifically for the return of the luggage. After much turmoil of mind and struggle in prayer, I concluded that I had every right to pray that somehow the writing that I had done for this book, which was in the suitcase, would be recovered even though the other content might be lost. So, I began to pray specifically and confidently for the recovery of the manscuript.

Within a week my luggage was found in a basement room of the hotel where I had stayed in New York. It had been stolen out of the room where the hotel clerk had left it. A valuable tape recorder and camera were missing. My manuscript was in tact and I could rejoice. My prayer had been purified and focused on that which deeply mattered. I prayed with confidence. I expected and received an answer.

REFLECTING AND RECORDING

Think about the attitude or expectation of your prayers.

Do you expect a response from God?

Do you ever consider the possibility that you may be praying *amiss?*

Do you stay with your praying long enough and with enough openness to God that your desire may be purified by the Spirit?

Does the way you pray ever change while you are praying?

Ponder these questions for a few minutes.

Here is a contemporary prayer of James Carroll. Now make it your own:

God, in our worried hearts we hide often from You
and from each other in old anxieties.
We forget that smiles at all the simple joys
are the surest signs of your being here.
You have given us a world full of children
and a night-time full of laughing stars.
The message is so simple we may miss it;
You are here in all of our everything:
in relief at windows hit and still unbroken,
in arguments ended at last in embracing,
in happy shocks of understanding between men.
Remind us, Lord, with strange seizures of joy
that these hates and wars and widowed hearts,
these moans of our time are exceptional.
Remind us, Lord, with ordinary happiness
That You have overcome all worlds of grief
and even now are wrapping us in coats
of common daily happenings of goodness.
Strip us, Lord, of melancholy strangeness,

for we accept Your word, not that misery
is unreal or painless, but that all of life
is quick, shot through with You and therefore,
fundamentally, with miles and smiles of joy.[5]

DURING THE DAY

On page 151 there are three copies of Isaiah 43:1-3 with blank spaces. Use each of those to write the name of one of the persons you selected on Day Two of this week for whom you have been praying. If you feel comfortable doing so, clip those copies from the workbook and send them to these friends, with a letter sharing with them your excitement about being personally loved by God. Tell them in your letter that you love and care and are praying for them.

DAY SEVEN
Jesus, Our Prayer Example

The parables of our Lord were just that—word pictures that teach great truths in story. Even so, his parables were not contrived; they came out of life. You may have identified Jesus as the caring shepherd looking for the lost sheep or as the good Samaritan stopping to attend to the wounded on the roadside. But have you ever put him in the place of the poor, unfortunate man out in the middle of the night knocking on a neighbor's door for bread? Don't read further until you think about that.

Imagine that as a child full of fear Jesus had lain in bed listening to the pounding on the door and the pleading call from without until his father, Joseph, got up and gave the man the bread for which he begged. Was it his own vivid experience he was recalling?

And did he remember that experience throughout his life when he was in the position of that midnight visitor, calling on God to give him the bread he needed?

And in the morning, a great while before day, he rose and went out to a lonely place, and there he prayed.

(Mark 1:35, RSV)

But he withdrew to the wilderness and prayed.

(Luke 5:16, RSV)

> In these days he went out into the hills to pray; and all night he continued in prayer to God.
>
> (Luke 6:12, RSV)

Jesus was an importunate pray-er!

Alexander Whyte painted the picture with powerful words:

> He continued all night. Do you see Him? Do you hear Him? Can you make out what He is asking? He stands up. He kneels down. He falls on His face. He knocks at the thick darkness. All that night He prays, and refuses to faint, till the sun rises, and He descends to His disciples like a strong man to run a race. And in Gethsemane all His past experiences in prayer, and all He had ever said to His disciples about prayer,—all that came back to His mind till His sweat was as it were great drops of blood falling to the ground. No,—we have not an high priest who cannot be touched with the feeling of our infirmities. ''Who in the days of His flesh, when He had offered up prayers and supplications with strong crying and tears . . . And being made perfect, He became the author of eternal salvation unto all them that obey Him.'' And in nothing more than in importunate prayer. [6]

REFLECTING AND RECORDING

Jesus said to Simon Peter, ''Simon, Simon, behold, Satan demanded to have you, that he might sift you like wheat, but I have prayed for you that your faith may not fail'' (Luke 22:31-32, RSV).

Spend a few minutes thinking about what that would have meant to you had you been Peter, and had you known as Peter did the person of prayer whom Jesus was.

Many persons find it helpful to keep a prayer list. Most of us naturally pray for members of our families and maybe close friends. But even this is often haphazard, without intention and intensity. A prayer list helps us to be focused and prevents forgetting.

The prayer list should change as conditions and situations change. Most of us can not pray for too many people or concerns at once, therefore we continually update our list—adding and deleting as we are led.

Page 153 is a Prayer List blank for you to use during this adventure. There are two categories: ongoing and immediate. In the ongoing column write the names of the persons who are sharing this study with you, as well as others, family, etc. for whom you pray regularly. Also list any ongoing special concerns you may have, e.g., your church, world peace, the poor. Pray for these now.

In the coming days we will consider the bold promise of scripture that Jesus ''ever liveth to make intercession'' for us (Hebrews 7:25, KJV). Claim whatever meaning that promise has for you now and thank God for the witness of Jesus as a person of prayer.

DURING THE DAY

Go through the day with this question: If Jesus' need for prayer was so great, can my need be less?

> For the group meeting: Provide one 3 x 5 card and a pencil for each person in the group.

GROUP MEETING FOR WEEK TWO

INTRODUCTION

Participation in a group such as this is a covenant relationship. You will profit most as you keep the daily discipline of the twenty- to thirty-minute period and as you faithfully attend these weekly meetings. Do not feel guilty if you have to miss a day in the workbook or be discouraged if you are not able to give the full twenty to thirty minutes in daily discipline. Don't hesitate sharing that with the group. We may learn something about ourselves as we share. We may discover, for instance, that we are unconsciously afraid of spending that time "alone with God" because of what he may reveal to us or require of us. Be patient with yourself and always be open to what God may be seeking to teach you.

A lot of our growth hinges upon our group participation. So share as openly and honestly as you can. Listen to what persons are saying. Sometimes there is meaning beyond the surface of their words which you may pick up if you are really attentive.

Being a sensitive participant in this fashion is crucial. Responding immediately to the feelings we pick up is also crucial. Sometimes it is important for the group to focus its entire attention upon a particular individual. If some need or concern is expressed, it may be appropriate for the leader to ask the group to enter into a brief period of special prayer for the persons or concerns revealed. Participants should not always depend upon the leader for this kind of sensitivity, for the leader may miss it. Even if you aren't the leader, don't hesitate to ask the group to join you in special prayer. This praying may be silent, or some person may wish to lead the group in prayer.

Remember, you have a contribution to make to the group. What you consider trivial or unimportant may be just what another person needs to hear. We are not seeking to be profound, but simply to share our experience.

SHARING TOGETHER

1. Begin your time together with the entire group praying aloud in unison Psalm 63 printed on Day One of this week. Follow this by singing the doxology:

> Praise God from whom all blessings flow;
> Praise Him, all creatures here below;
> Praise Him above, ye heavenly host:
> Praise Father, Son, and Holy Ghost. Amen.
>
> THOMAS KEN

2. Let each person share the most meaningful day in this week's workbook adventure.

3. Now share the most difficult day and tell why it was difficult.

4. A great affirmation of scripture and a key to effective prayer is *God loves me.* Let persons in the group who will, share their responses to this affirmation. Do you believe it? How have you experienced it? What prevents you from believing and experiencing it? (You may spend as much as fifteen minutes sharing at this point.)

5. Assuming that not many of us have an adequate prayer life, let as many persons as will, share honestly why they feel they do not pray as they should.

PRAYING TOGETHER

On Day Seven of this week you were asked to put the names of each person in your group on your prayer list. An important part of this adventure is the members praying for each other daily. During these sharing sessions you may wish to make some notes that will help you recall specific concerns related to each individual. These notes will assist you in praying for persons in a focused way.

1. The leader will distribute a 3 x 5 card and pencil to each participant and describe how they are to be used: "We are a prayer community. We are at different places in our understanding, commitment, and practice. Yet, each of us has a basic interest and commitment or we would not be here. On the card you have been given write your name, and one need in your life which you are willing for another person in this group to know and pray about. The cards will be collected and then randomly distributed, so you need to share something that you would be willing for any person in this group to know about. It may or may not be something you have already shared. After the cards have been redistributed, we will then have a period of silent prayer for the needs expressed. You will take the card that has been given you and pray daily for the need expressed."

(Let the group prepare their cards, and the leader receive them, shuffle them, redistribute them, then ask for a period of silent prayer . . . two or three minutes. Remind the group to put this special concern on their prayer list begun on Day Seven.) Note: Inform all participants that these cards should be brought to the next meeting.

2. Enter into a period of sharing verbal prayer by allowing each person to mention any special needs they wish to share with the entire group. They may want to share some of the names they recorded on Day Two of this week and those who need to know they are loved by God.

A good pattern is to ask for a period of prayer after each need is mentioned. There may be silent prayer by the entire group, or someone may offer a brief two- or three-sentence verbal prayer.

3. Close your time by praying together the great prayer of the church, "Our Father." As you pray this prayer, remember that you are linking yourselves with all Christians of all time in universal intercession.

WORDS OF ENCOURAGEMENT

As you begin this third week of your journey, here are some thoughts to keep in mind.

Discipline is an important dimension of life. Discipline is not slavish rigidity, but an ordering of life that enables you to be the master of your circumstances, rather than controlled by them. For most people, a designated time of prayer is essential for building a life of prayer.

If you have not yet established a regular time as your "prayer time," try to find the right time for you this week. Experiment: In the morning, after work, during the lunch hour, before retiring, find the time that seems best for you.

If you discover that you can't cover all the workbook material and exercises given for a day, don't berate yourself. Get what you can out of what you do. There is no point in rushing over three or four steps or principles if you cannot think deeply. Pray seriously about them one by one.

Intellectual assent to a great principle or possibility is important, but it does us little good until we act upon it—until we say yes in our minds.

Don't hesitate to make decisions and resolves, but don't condemn yourself if you fail. God is patient, and he wants us to be patient with ourselves.

Overcoming Some Hurdles 3

DAY ONE
Intimidated by Science and Technology

There are so many questions about prayer, so much confusion, so much doubt. The nature of this workbook experience does not allow us to deal at length or in depth with all the questions and doubts. However, there are some specific hurdles we must overcome if we would pray—especially if we are to be serious about intercessory prayer. The first is *our intimidation by science and technology.* In past generations prayer itself has not been a problem. The problem was what kinds of prayer? or discipline? or perseverance? or technique?

Today it is different. We have a modern mentality, shaped by science and technology, which causes some persons to question the meaning and authenticity of prayer. Freudian analysis, scientific determinism, the process of secularization, along with the almost unbelievable accomplishments of science and technology have for many emptied the universe of its spiritual meaning. In such a universe, defined and explained by science, prayer appears alien to our natural human life.

The truth is that most of us, consciously or unconsciously, are intimidated by science and technology. Even though the urge to pray is still present and the tendency to reach out in prayer to and for others is very real, we are timid and uncertain over our commitment. The basic problem is that in the way science has defined man and the universe, God is *apart from,* if at all. Brother Pierre-Yves Emery of the Taize Community in France has given the best explanation I know regarding an answer to this scientific mentality:

> Science and technology have taught us to experience the world as having its own consistency, an internal coherence, and a harmony of laws which can be known, anticipated, and often modified. The universe seems to be autonomous, developing out itself. . . .
>
> What is true of the universe is also true of man. This truth is experienced in mankind's increasing power, its immense responsibility, its freedom, as well as in the weight of its history. This is the autonomy of mankind, in a relative sense at least, and the coherence of the psychological and sociological processes that fashion it.

Without in any way detracting from science's value and possibilities and without disowning the intellectual attitude that science requires, we must accept the importance of not making it a new myth. This grows from respect for what science is. Science is not the only approach to reality, for the simple reason that the method of science is abstraction, the use of statistics, and the artificial separating out from all reality the area chosen for investigation. This is perfectly legitimate if one does not forget that, since it proceeds from abstraction, scientific knowledge remains partial and limited. In particular, the scientific method abstracts God from reality, an abstraction that is legitimate and necessary. But science should not overtly take this methodological principle for a scientific conclusion. Science has nothing to say about God because it disqualifies itself at the outset.[7]

I call this hurdle to your attention now, because we need to bring it to conscious awareness. We cannot deal with it thoroughly in this experiment, but we will be conscious of it and hopefully gain some insight.

The key is to see science and technology for what they are: valuable but limited by their own decision to deal with a certain part of reality. Also, we must see that the dimension of reality with which we deal in religion is just as real. God is not separated from the reality of science. Science may seek to make God so in its scientific methodology. But God is not limited, either by persons or the world. Though the world and humankind have a consistency and a certain autonomy of their own, God is not merely complementary to humankind and the world. *God is necessary.*

God is not a stopgap to explain phenomena not yet understood. Yet we make that mistake in the church—projecting an image of a stopgap God, one whom we focus on when we are without a rational explanation. God is at the heart of life and the universe, the cause for their being and the dynamic for their consistency, autonomy, and ongoingness.

We need not therefore be intimidated by science! Hopefully the essential reality with which we will be dealing in this adventure in prayer, and the sharpened focus of our own self-awareness, will make us bold in pursuing the possibility of prayer—mysterious though it may be.

REFLECTING AND RECORDING

Could it be that the problem of prayer today is not a problem of prayer itself, but the way we understand the world and humankind? Ponder these questions: Is my prayer a part of my whole life or something apart from reality as I perceive it? Do I believe that my praying makes a difference?

One wonders whether the person who wrote Psalm 8 would have been intimidated by our modern science and technology. In an extravagant boldness he saw himself (humankind) and God in beautiful perspective. Spend as much time as you have left in this period reflecting upon this integrated picture of reality.

Read it as often as you wish for meaning and content, then read it once as your own prayer.

O Lord, our Lord,
  how majestic is thy name in all the earth!
Thou whose glory above the heavens is chanted
  by the mouth of babes and infants,
thou hast founded a bulwark because of thy foes,
  to still the enemy and the avenger.

When I look at thy heavens, the work of thy fingers,
  the moon and the stars which thou hast established;
what is man that thou art mindful of him,
  and the son of man that thou dost care for him?
Yet thou hast made him little less than God,
  and dost crown him with glory and honor.
Thou hast given him dominion over the works of thy hands;
  thou hast put all things under his feet,
all sheep and oxen,
  and also the beasts of the field,
the birds of the air, and the fish of the sea,
  whatever passes along the paths of the sea.

O Lord, our Lord,
  how majestic is thy name in all the earth!
                    (Psalm 8, RSV)

DURING THE DAY

As you move through the different segments of the day, consciously raise these questions: Is God a part of this hunk of reality? What is the meaning of prayer in relation to what I am doing—or, what is the meaning of what I am doing in relation to God and prayer?

DAY TWO
Natural Law and God's Intervention

A second hurdle we must overcome may be captioned *natural law and God's intervention*. When we practice intercessory prayer, we are calling for God's intervention. How can we expect such intervention in light of the apparent uniformity of natural law.

This is the picture. Certain causes operating under certain conditions always lead to certain results. Thus, science has discovered and used the laws of cause and effect to predict the future and to develop and control energy. The incredible technological and scientific progress we have made has been possible because we live in a law-abiding universe.

The question has been prominent, though there are bountiful signs of its diminishing: How can we expect God to interrupt the natural laws which he has put into operation, laws which make human existence possible and insure our well-being?

On the surface at least, it seems that is what we do when we practice intercession. We are asking God to intervene into the apparent natural course of cause and effect.

Actually that is not the case altogether. Science has discovered and is acknowledging that natural law is not so invariable as was once supposed. A great latitude of uncertainty is recognized. Natural laws are human descriptions of the ordinarily regular sequences of nature. Henry Bett has given perspective to this understanding of natural law.

> It is perfectly obvious, when you think it out, that a law of nature is merely a statement as to the normal behavior of things in particular conditions; no more and no less. It does not ordain that things should happen thus; it does not compel things to happen thus; it simply states that normally things do happen thus. It is a statement of uniformity with definite limits, based upon observation, and expressed in metrical terms. As to why things behave in that regular way, or what makes things behave in that regular way, a natural law cannot tell you anything at all.[8]

The question, then, becomes one of *our* using and *God's* using the orderly ways of nature to accomplish his purpose.

Occasionally, an answer to prayer appears to violate natural law. We celebrate that not because it is spectacular, but because we know we simply do not understand all God's laws. We believe that God responds to our prayers to accomplish his purposive will. The truth is that God is always intervening. "Special interventions" may appear paradoxical. We can live with the paradoxes as we realize that God interacts with all that is, not necessarily suspending natural laws, but working within the freedom that exists within natural laws. In prayer we add our receptivity to God's interventions.

REFLECTING AND RECORDING

The following is one of the most dramatic accounts of God's interventions in nature experienced by Moses and the Israelites as they fled their Egyptian captors:

> Then the angel of God who went before the host of Israel moved and went behind them; and the pillar of cloud moved from before them and stood behind them, coming between the host of Egypt and the host of Israel. And there was the cloud and the darkness; and the night passed without one coming near the other all night.
>
> Then Moses stretched out his hand over the sea; and the Lord drove the sea back by a strong east wind all night, and made the sea dry land, and the waters were divided. And the people of Israel went into the midst of the sea on dry ground, the waters being a wall to them on their right hand and on their left. The Egyptians pursued, and went in after them into the midst of the sea, all Pharaoh's horses, his chariots, and his horsemen. And in the morning watch the Lord in the

pillar of fire and of cloud looked down upon the host of the Egyptians, and discomfited the host of the Egyptians, clogging their chariot wheels so that they drove heavily; and the Egyptians said, "Let us flee from before Israel; for the Lord fights for them against the Egyptians."

Then the Lord said to Moses, "Stretch out your hand over the sea, that the water may come back upon the Egyptians, upon their chariots, and upon their horsemen." So Moses stretched forth his hand over the sea, and the sea returned to its wonted flow when the morning appeared; and the Egyptians fled into it, and the Lord routed the Egyptians in the midst of the sea. The waters returned and covered the chariots and the horsemen and all the host of Pharaoh that had followed them into the sea; not so much as one of them remained. But the people of Israel walked on dry ground through the sea, the waters being a wall to them on their right hand and on their left.

Thus the Lord saved Israel that day from the hand of the Egyptians; and Israel saw the Egyptians dead upon the seashore. And Israel saw the great work which the Lord did against the Egyptians, and the people feared the Lord; and they believed in the Lord and in his servant Moses.

(Exodus 14:19-31, RSV).

Let your mind be flexible. Be reflective and without looking for the super dramatic, examine your own history. Can you recall an experience when *on the surface* it seemed that natural laws were interrupted in answer to your prayer? Record your experience here.

Name the experience._____

_____

_____

Locate the experience in time._____

Which natural law was involved?_____

What was your conclusion then?_____

_____

What is your conclusion now?_____

_____

Are you using your prayer list? Do you need to update it?

DURING THE DAY

We want to get into the habit of "flashing" prayers at every reminder of need. Begin today to flash prayers when you see an accident, hear a fire or ambulance siren, see police rushing to a call, pass a hospital or a school. Let the occasions for "flash prayers" grow as a personal practice as you become more and more sensitive to needs for prayer.

DAY THREE
Human Freedom/God's Intervention

The third hurdle on the path of intercessory prayer has to do with **God's intervention (or, more strongly, interference) in the exercise of human freedom.** Human freedom is one of the central tenets of the Christian faith. The question is: what happens to human freedom when God responds to intercessory prayer?

When we pray for others, we are seeking to influence them by calling upon God to act in their lives. As I am working on this question, my oldest child, Kim, is a senior in high school. She is in the process of choosing her vocation and the college she will attend. These decisions are crucial and will play a huge role in her future. While she doesn't have to make a specific vocational choice now, very soon she will have to select a college.

Where Kim goes to college is very important. She will, in all likelihood, make her vocational choice in that setting. She will get much of the intellectual grounding for her values and commitments. Her commitments will be shaped and sharpened. She probably will meet the person she will marry. It is no wonder that I am praying that God will play a role in Kim's decision. The question: How is this affecting Kim's freedom of choice?

Human freedom. As much as we affirm and defend this distinctive characteristic of humankind (we are not puppets, but free children of God!), still there is no such thing as *complete* human freedom. The actual freedom we know exists within limits, limits which have been determined by many factors beyond our control: where, when, and to whom we were born; physical strength; intellectual endowments; educational and social opportunities.

Also, we may expand or limit our freedom by the choices we make, by the way we use the freedom we already possess. We may choose to live unselfishly for God, or selfishly for ourselves. We may choose to be disciplined in learning and growing spiritually, or we may be lazy, letting our minds drift and our spirits float aimlessly.

The point is that our freedom is a variable factor, existing in limits a part of which we have determined and a part of which may be determined by factors beyond our control.

Intercessory prayer may be included in these factors. When I pray for Kim I am asking God to bring certain influences to bear upon her life. I am not making a choice for her nor praying that her freedom be violated, but that she be open to God and be given a broader perspective for her *new freedom of choice.*

Because I love Kim—love her enough to pray earnestly for her—God is able to present opportunities and alternatives of which Kim may otherwise be unaware.

REFLECTING AND RECORDING

The psalmist knew the illuminating presence of God in his life, affirming, "For with thee is the fountain of life; in thy light do we see light" (Psalm 36:9, RSV).

Read this affirmation aloud slowly and deliberately:

Thy steadfast love, O Lord, extends to the heavens;
　thy faithfulness to the clouds.
Thy righteousness is like the mountains of God,
　thy judgments are like the great deep;
　man and beast thou savest, Lord.
How precious is thy steadfast love, O God!
　The children of men take refuge in the shadow of thy wings.
They feast on the abundance of thy house,
　and thou givest them drink from the river of thy delights.
For with thee is the fountain of life;
　in thy light do we see light.
　　　　　(Psalm 36:5-9, RSV)

So, the truth is we pray for another that the light of God will be given, that God's light will be seen, and in God's light right choices made.

Now repeat that last affirmation of the psalm aloud four or five times:

For with thee is the fountain of life;
　in thy light do we see light.

DURING THE DAY

On page 155 you will find the above affirmation printed. If you have not memorized it, clip it out and take it with you today. Now and then, in moments when you can be quiet and reflective, read it and make it your personal affirmation.

DAY FOUR
A Subtle Temptation: Did God Really Act?

The two previous days we have considered God's *intervention.* Yesterday we thought about God's presenting new opportunities and alternatives to others, opportunities and alternatives which they might not otherwise be aware of. This is all in the framework of the person's freedom to choose.

It is also true that guidance is provided in the same fashion: a right path may be chosen, danger may be revealed and averted, closed paths may be opened, persons may escape trouble—all as a result of our praying. God's answer is not a violation of freedom, but the offer of new ways, new relationships, new answers.

REFLECTING AND RECORDING

Think back over the past few days or weeks and locate an occasion when, as a result of your praying, a completely new direction was given or a new alternative was opened. Briefly record that experience here.

In a few sentences describe a situation in which you prayed for another, the way you prayed, and how you perceive your prayers were received.

If you have not had such an experience, think of an experience about which you know, perhaps an experience someone else has shared with you. Make a brief note of the experience.

Here is another hurdle to overcome: the gnawing question, *Did God really do this?*

This is the subtle temptation to doubt which creeps in upon us when we think about answered prayer. C. S. Lewis in his satirical *Screwtape Letters*

3

has pictured this. Screwtape, the devil's advocate, writes to his nephew, instructing him on ways to lead Christians astray. In the matter of answered prayer, he counseled planting seeds of doubt in potential victims. Get the person doubting. "If the thing he prays for doesn't happen, then that is one more proof that petitionary prayers don't work; if it does happen, he will, of course, be able to see some of the physical causes that led up to it, and therefore it would have happened anyway, and thus a granted prayer becomes just as good as a denied one that prayers are ineffective." [9]

Almost always, especially as we begin to take intercession seriously, there is the subtle temptation to doubt, and this is a hurdle we must overcome. It's a waste of time to try to prove that prayers are answered. The proof is within ourselves and in our own religious experience. Rufus Jones has stated it beautifully: ". . . those of us who pray have the best of all evidence that prayer is a vital breath of life, for we come back from it quickened and vitalized, refreshed and restored, and we are happy to believe and trust that our intercourse with the companion of our lives has helped to fill with love the cup which some friend of ours with agonizing hands was holding up in some hour of need." [10]

REFLECTING AND RECORDING

Look again at what you recorded above as answered prayer. Thank God for it and ask him to deliver you (even ahead of time) from doubting that he answers prayers.

DURING THE DAY

As you move through this day be sensitive to how God may be guiding you, how he may reveal danger, open a new door, close one . . . always giving you the choice.

DAY FIVE
If God Knows Everything, Why Pray?

Here is a challenging word from Jesus:

Beware of practicing your piety before men in order to be seen by them; for then you will have no reward from your Father who is in heaven.

Thus, when you give alms, sound no trumpet before you, as the hypocrites do in the synagogues and in the streets, that they may be praised by men. Truly, I say to you, they have their reward. But when you give alms, do not let your left hand know what your right hand is doing, so that your alms may be in secret; and your Father who sees in secret will reward you.

And when you pray, you must not be like the hypocrites; for they love to stand and pray in the synagogues and at the street corners, that they may be seen by men. Truly, I say to you, they have their reward. But when you pray, go into your room and shut the door and pray to your Father who is in secret; and your Father who sees in secret will reward you.

And in praying do not heap up empty phrases as the Gentiles do; for they think that they will be heard for their many words. Do not be like them, for your Father knows what you need before you ask him. . . .

(Matthew 6:1-8, RSV)

As indicated earlier this week, there are some legitimate questions which arise as we seek to make the case for prayer. Here is a common one: *If God knows everything, why pray?* This is another hurdle. Jesus affirmed that our Father knows what we need even before we ask him. Then why ask at all?

We can't say these things too often: Intercessory prayer is not an effort on our part to put pressure on God; nor is it an effort to twist destiny in our favor or according to our will; nor is it a matter of advising God. Having said that, the question may still clamor for an answer: *Why pray?*

Brother Pierre-Yves Emery, whom I quoted earlier, has stated the fundamental reason for intercession so clearly:

It expresses, in a very authentic way, what it first obliges us to recognize: that in our relationship with God we have no rights, nothing is due us; it is a relationship of grace. Miracle does not exist only in the extraordinary; it also exists—and is more widely present—in all the good that happens to us in the usual course of things. The facts that we exist and that God loves us cannot be taken for granted. Prayers of petition express, with simplicity, this attitude which alone can respond to the generosity of God, an attitude of admiring astonishment, of humble recognition, and of love.[11]

That we are completely dependent upon God is a beautiful realization. So we pray. The relationship between us and God is one of grace. There is also this added reason for intercession which we considered during the first week of our adventure: *God truly counts on our prayers.* We don't understand it, and, until we see God face to face, it will remain a mystery. But miracle of miracles, that's the way it is: *God's design includes our participation.* So Brother Pierre-Yves concludes:

We can well ask ourselves what good our prayer can do—not to mention our faith and our actions—within the secret, hidden way in which God makes all things work together for the good of those who love him, and for the final transfiguration of the creation. But we may not give up believing and saying that truly our prayer, by the power of the Spirit of God in us, is itself like a power that plays its role in the plan of God.[12]

REFLECTING AND RECORDING

The following affirmations come from the above statements of Brother Pierre-Yves Emery. Spend a couple of minutes reflecting on each of these truths and seek to discover for yourself their deep meaning.

In our relationship with God we have no rights; it is a relationship of grace.

Miracle exists not only in the extraordinary, but is more widely present in all the good that happens in the normal course of things.

We must not take God's love for granted. Our petitions to him are an expression of our humble recognition and astonishment at his love.

Our prayer is part of the plan of God to work good for those who love him.

Now write your prayer using the above affirmations as a framework for expressing yourself to God.

DURING THE DAY

As you go through the day, look for the miracles that will come to you and others in the *ordinary goodness* you experience.

DAY SIX
The Integrity of Intercession Without Action

"Not to work and then to pray to make up for it I consider to be bad manners." That word of Charles Péguy makes the point by understatement. To seek to make up for work by praying is not only bad manners, it is bad religion. In fact, it is unchristian.

We will consider the harmony of intercession and action in Week Seven. For now, however, this is a hurdle to overcome. There are occasions which call us to pray when we know that there is no opportunity to act ourselves. Can my intercessions have integrity in such cases? Is it honest to pray when I know I will not be able to interject myself into the situation or be in relation to the person for whom I pray?

The answer is an unequivocal yes—and it rests on our confidence in the power of God. At the heart of all prayer, and certainly intercession, is our willingness to be at God's disposal, to be available for any action to which he calls us. We must not, however, limit our prayers to that which is within the apparent reach of our personal action.

Huub Oosterhuis has given us a powerful picture of praying as a way of living, of waiting, of keeping the door open. The picture was given during the Vietnam War.

> We cannot, all of us, make peace in Vietnam come true. We still cannot—we are caught up in schemes, the need for an armament industry linked to the economic process, the balance of power in Southeast Asia, all those gods, all those sticks to beat us with. But we try to believe that God is greater than schemes, that he is the Lord of all powers and gods.
>
> Sometimes I think that demonstrating for peace in Vietnam, doing something concrete like joining in a march, really has something to do with faith and with prayer. Maybe this sort of protest is a desperate attempt to keep the case open everywhere in the world. Somewhere, a thousand or so people who don't know what to God they ought to do just begin to walk in order to show that it could be different, that we, a bunch of people, a thousand or so marching, are greater and more eternal than the war.
>
> There are people who feel this way about it; protest is born in them. They are the poor in spirit. All appearance and all reason is against them. What sort of influence can their marching have, in God's name, on events in the world? Well, precisely the same influence as prayer, I think. When we pray in the liturgy, together with others in our congregations, for peace, we associate ourselves with this kind of fruitless demonstration. Appearances and reason are against us, too—what happens to prayer like that? But just imagine if we were to give up asking for peace, just like that, desperately or naively? We would probably become choked up ourselves, shut up like clams. So we say, let us pray. We keep the door open to the possibility of peace, of a new creation. We open our minds to the possibility that it *is* something—grace.[13]

Who knows? Can we ever be absolutely sure there is "nothing we can do"? So we pray, even when it appears that direct action is not possible. We pray for a friend a thousand miles away. We pray for peace and justice. We pray for prison reform. We pray always *ready* to act—and often our praying brings us back to immediate concrete situations around us, and we act there, still believing that our prayers make a difference in situations where we can't act.

REFLECTING AND RECORDING:

To believe that our praying makes a difference, and to pray even when it seems that we cannot act is to link ourselves with Christ in his ongoing intercession. Consider this claim of scripture: "The former priests were many in number, because they were prevented by death from continuing in office; but he holds his priesthood permanently, because he continues for ever. Consequently he is able for all time to save those who draw near to God through him, since he always lives to make intercession for them" (Hebrews 7:23-25, RSV).

Spend a few minutes pondering the thought that Jesus always lives to make intercession for us.

Deliberately now, think of some person or need in which it seems impossible for you to act. List them here.

A person you can pray for only_____

A need you can pray for only_____

Pray for them. In a deliberate way offer them to Jesus, the great intercessor.

Look at your prayer list. Is who or what you have been praying for presently on that list? If not, you may wish to place it there. Examine your list to see if and how many concerns are there for which, it appears, you may never have the opportunity to act. If there are none, put at least one person or concern on your list. In the days ahead, as you pray for these needs for which you think you cannot act, be especially attentive to whether some avenue of action, involvement, or relationship is opened to you.

DURING THE DAY

Anticipate three or four occasions during the day when you can pray, however briefly, for the person or need you have just been centering upon. Deciding now that you will do so will reinforce the possibility of remembering to do so. Occasions may be stops at traffic lights, coffee break, waiting for an appointment, thanksgiving before meals, etc.

Write your chosen occasions here:

1._____

2._____

3._____

4._____

DAY SEVEN
Intercession: Struggle or Surrender?

So the men turned from there, and went toward Sodom; but Abraham still stood before the Lord. Then Abraham drew near, and said, "Wilt thou indeed destroy the righteous with the wicked? Suppose there are fifty righteous within the city; wilt thou then destroy the place and not spare it for the fifty righteous who are in it? Far be it from thee to do such a thing, to slay the righteous with the wicked, so that the righteous fare as the wicked! Far be that from thee! Shall not the Judge of all the earth do right?" And the Lord said, "If I find at Sodom fifty righteous in the city, I will spare the whole place for their sake." Abraham answered, "Behold, I have taken upon myself to speak to the Lord, I who am but dust and ashes. Suppose five of the fifty righteous are lacking? Wilt thou destroy the whole city for lack of five? And he said, "I will not destroy it if I find forty-five there." Again he spoke to him, and said, "Suppose forty are found there." He answered, "For the sake of forty I will not do it." Then he said, "Oh let not the Lord be angry, and I will speak. Suppose thirty are found there." He answered, "I will not do it, if I find thirty there." He said, "Behold, I have taken upon myself to speak to the Lord. Suppose twenty are found there." He answered, "For the sake of twenty I will not destroy it." Then he said, "Oh let not the Lord be angry, and I will speak again but this once. Suppose ten are found there." He answered, "For the sake of ten I will not destroy it." And the Lord went his way, when he had finished speaking to Abraham; and Abraham returned to his place.
(Genesis 18:22-33, RSV)

In this scripture we have a dramatic example of Old Testament intercession. We may look at the passage as too literal. We may have difficulty thinking of such a graphic exchange between a person and God. Try to set aside that kind of difficulty and try to feel the struggle going on within Abraham. The question is raised, *Is intercessory prayer a struggle—a persevering like the "friend at midnight" or the "widow before the judge"?*

Is intercessory prayer *a struggle not against God, but against adversity or the forces of evil?*

Paul urged the Ephesians to struggle in prayer: "Pray at all times in the Spirit, with all prayer and supplication. To that end keep alert with all perseverance, making supplication for all the saints'' (Ephesians 6:18, RSV).

Yet, if prayer is an experience into which we enter in an effort to make God's will our will, might we not best describe intercession as *surrender*? Again, Pierre-Yves Emery, to whom I owe a great debt of gratitude for teaching me so much about prayer, has put the tension clearly:

> . . . The image of struggle, the emphasis on earnest perseverance, certainly expresses faith, in that it makes the believer an intimate of God. But it is a short step from prayer as wrestling with God to prayer as a means of pressure or an act of magic. We find it so easy to make God into a satellite of a center that is ourselves.
>
> But there is an opposite risk, more common in our time. Confident surrender can hide a certain skepticism, can express a vague faith in God, who is distant or somewhere else. Do we dare to trust the promises of God, to count ardently on the seriousness of his commitment to us, *to appeal from God to God in the name of his love,* [italics mine] as Abraham did before Sodom and Gomorrah? Or do we experience prayer so well distilled that it is almost nonexistent? Almost as if we hardly dare to stand by what we ask.
>
> Our intercession must always oscillate somewhat beween these two emphases. Faith is simultaneously long perseverance and unwavering confidence. If prayer is too much involved with insisting, it no longer addresses itself to the true God; if it is too quickly and too easily confident, it no longer expresses us truly.[14]

We must keep a rhythm in our intercession—a rhythm between persevering struggle and confident surrender. In this rhythm we move to God and God moves to us.

REFLECTING AND RECORDING

Recall and describe here a personal experience of intercession in which you struggled and persevered with God.

Describe a personal experience of intercession you characterize as confident surrender.

There is a sense in which answer to prayer is always certain. *Even when God cannot answer affirmatively a person's petition, he can answer the person.* If God cannot answer the petition and change the circumstances, he supplies sufficient power to overcome them. He answers either the petition or the person.

Pray now that you will begin to be able to sense and practice this rhythm of struggle and surrender; that you will be aware when God is answering *you,* though not granting your petition.

If you are in a group, your meeting will be sometime today. Pray that you will be ready to contribute to the meeting, and that this meeting will contribute to each person's growth. Be sure to take the 3 x 5 card you received last week to the meeting tonight.

DURING THE DAY

Work to sense and practice the rhythm of struggle and surrender. Be aware when God is answering you, though not granting your petition.

GROUP MEETING FOR WEEK THREE

INTRODUCTION

Feedback in your group meeting is necessary to keep the group dynamic working positively for all participants. The leader should be sensitive to this. Persons should be encouraged to share their feelings about how the group is functioning. Begin this session by asking for feedback.

Checking meaning by feedback is also essential for communication. We often mishear what a person is saying. A simple practice of feeding back to the person what you have heard (e.g., "I hear you saying that you have to force yourself to pray. Is that it?") will enhance communication.

This has significant meaning in prayer. We want to know that we are being heard. To be heard by our friends may be the first step in our experience of God as a friend who really hears! So, each of us should practice listening, also feeding back to check meaning in order that our fellow prayer-pilgrims may know that we really hear. It takes only one or two persons attempting this kind of serious listening to set the mood for the entire group.

Begin this session by encouraging feedback.

SHARING TOGETHER

1. Spend fifteen or twenty minutes talking about "hurdles." Which hurdles have you had difficulty with? Did the text raise questions you have not faced before? How do you feel about that kind of probing? Members of the group may help, clarify questions that are still bothering someone in the group.

2. Ask persons who are willing to share experiences of
—"being led"
—or receiving direction
—or being given a new alternative as they reflected upon Day
   Four of this week.

3. Ask some person to read aloud the quote from Rufus Jones on Day Four. Spend some time talking about this statement as the final answer to your difficulties and hurdles in prayer.

4. Ask persons to share experiences of intercession as struggle and surrender, and the result of that intercession.

PRAYING TOGETHER

1. Begin your time of praying together by dividing into two groups across the room from each other. Share responsively the following prayer/litany from Psalm 136.

Group one: O give thanks to the Lord, for he is good,
Group two: *for his steadfast love endures for ever.*

Group one: O give thanks to the God of gods,
Group two: *for his steadfast love endures for ever.*

Group one: O give thanks to the Lord of lords,
Group two: *for his steadfast love endures for ever;*

Group one: to him who alone does great wonders,
Group two: *for his steadfast love endures for ever;*

Group one: to him who by understanding made the heavens,
Group two: *for his steadfast love endures for ever;*

Group one: to him who spread out the earth upon the waters,
Group two: *for his steadfast love endures for ever;*

Group one: to him who made the great lights,
Group two: *for his steadfast love endures for ever;*

Group one: the sun to rule over the day,
Group two: *for his steadfast love endures for ever;*

Group one: the moon and stars to rule over the night;
Group two: *for his steadfast love endures for ever;*

Group one: to him who smote the first-born of Egypt,
Group two: *for his steadfast love endures for ever;*

Group one: and brought Israel out from among them,
Group two: *for his steadfast love endures for ever;*

Group one: with a strong hand and an outstretched arm,
Group two: *for his steadfast love endures for ever;*

Group one: to him who divided the Red Sea in sunder,
Group two: *for his steadfast love endures for ever;*

Group one: and made Israel pass through the midst of it,
Group two: *for his steadfast love endures for ever;*

Group one: but overthrew Pharaoh and his host in the Red Sea,
Group two: *for his steadfast love endures for ever;*

Group one: to him who led his people through the wilderness,
Group two: *for his steadfast love endures for ever;*

Group one: and gave their land as a heritage,
Group two: *for his steadfast love endures for ever;*

Group one: a heritage to Israel his servant,
Group two: *for his steadfast love endures for ever.*

Group one: It is he who remembered us in our low estate,
Group two: for his steadfast love endures for ever;

Group one: and rescued us from our foes,
Group two: *for his steadfast love endures for ever;*

Group one: he who gives food to all flesh,
Group two: *for his steadfast love endures for ever.*

Group one: O give thanks to the God of heaven,
Group two: *for his steadfast love endures for ever.*

2. Leader, ask persons for 3 x 5 cards they received last week. If someone failed to bring his/her card, ask that the name and need be written on a new card. Shuffle and redistribute the cards, then spend a couple of minutes in silent prayer related to the concerns on the cards. (These cards will be kept by each participant for prayer attention during the coming week.)

3. The church, universal as well as our own local congregation, should receive our prayer attention. Sometimes we are inclined to think of the failures or problems of the church rather than her positive contribution to individuals, the community, and the world. Let each person in the group share at least one thing about the church for which he/she is grateful. Following this sharing let the entire group respond in unison, *"Lord, we thank you for the church."*

4. Now pray in unison this prayer for the church:

O God, we pray for Thy Church, which is set to-day amid the perplexities of a changing order, and face to face with a great new task. . . . Baptize her afresh in the life-giving spirit of Jesus! . . . Put upon her lips the ancient gospel of her Lord.

. . . Fill her with the prophets' scorn of tyranny, and with a Christlike tenderness for the heavyladen and down-trodden. . . . Bid her cease from seeking her own life, lest she lose it. Make her valiant to give up her life to humanity, that like her crucified Lord she may mount by the path of the cross to a higher glory.[15] Amen.

5. Leader close by praying a brief prayer that gathers up the mood of the sharing and the concerns that have been expressed.

Some Essential Principles of Intercession 4

DAY ONE
Who Are We to Tell God What to Do?

Today let's make a transition from the questions and hurdles we considered last week to some essential principles of intercession. Consider this promise:

> The Lord is near; have no anxiety, but in everything make your requests known to God in prayer and petition with thanksgiving. Then the peace of God, which is beyond our utmost understanding, will keep guard over your hearts and your thoughts, in Christ Jesus.
>
> (Philippians 4:6-7, NEB)

Have you ever considered the question, Who are we that we should tell God what to do? Shouldn't we believe that God is already ordering all things for the best? Probing questions, which, on the surface seem to negate the possibility of prayer making any difference in God's scheme of things. Not so!

Get this clear now: *Christian prayer is conscious communication with God. Prayer is not telling God what to do; it is rather sharing our needs with him.* It is making our requests known to him. As indicated yesterday, struggle and surrender are involved. There is great mystery here.

In the last resort we leave it to the wisdom of God to decide precisely what he is to do about our needs. We do not presume to tell him what to do, but we do not hesitate to share what our presumed needs are. And we do not stop believing that the very sharing of those needs plays a dynamic role in God's response.

To believe that God knows best and is ordering all things for the best doesn't cause us to cease working for the best God has for us. The stoic may submit to fate and not work for the fulfillment of the good, but not the Christian.

Likewise, our praying. Even though we may believe that God knows best and therefore is ordering what is best for our loved one, we do not cease to work for the loved one's recovery. We use every available means modern medicine has set at our disposal as well as all the love and psychological support we can give to enhance healing. Should the same case not be made for prayer? If it is right to *work* for a certain end, isn't it just as right to *pray* for that purpose? John Baillie states it succinctly: "Clearly we must not pray for any end towards which it is wrong to labour, but likewise we must not labour towards any end for which it is wrong to pray." [16]

On Day Three of last week I shared about my prayers for Kim and her selection of a college. Many weeks have passed since I wrote that, and I have continued to pray—and work. She has decided to go to Emory University. At one point in the selection process, Emory seemed out of the question, though it was Kim's first choice. The costs were too high. To abbreviate the story, two things have happened which I believe are results of our praying. One, after weeks of looking at other college catalogues and costs, I was led one day, out of prayer and a conversation with a friend, to reexamine the financial program we had worked on in relation to Emory. I discovered that I had included two figures twice in our cost analysis, and though still beyond our financial reach, the costs were not so great as we had figured. Two, I encouraged Kim to make application to Emory and to seek a scholarship even though we had been led to believe she would not be eligible. She received word about a month later, when her second-choice college was pressing her to make a commitment for enrollment, that Emory had granted her a $1,000 annual scholarship.

It is not that we tell God what to do; it is that we are God's children, created for relationship with him. God has invited us to share our needs with him. Indeed the working of God's will within us, and with others is often dependent upon our praying.

This is at least a partial answer to the question with which we began our adventure: "What if there are some things God either cannot or will not do until people pray?"

REFLECTING AND RECORDING

Is there a concern you have now in which it seems you are telling God what to do? Think about it and if so, write it here.

Are you praying for something for which you are not willing to labor? For a person with whom you are not willing to relate? Think about it, and if so, write it here.

Recall and record here a personal prayer experience similar to the one which I shared about Kim—one in which praying and working came together.

If you are in a group, think about the sharing in your weekly meeting yesterday. Write three or four needs which were expressed there and then pray about them.

DURING THE DAY

Philippians 4:6-7 is printed on page 155. Clip it out and carry it with you or put it in a place where you can read it often, e.g., tape it on your car dashboard or your refrigerator door. During this day try to commit it to memory.

DAY TWO
Urgent Need

> And he said to them, "Which of you who has a friend will go to him at midnight and say to him, 'Friend, lend me three loaves; for a friend of mine has arrived on a journey, and I have nothing to set before him': and he will answer from within, 'Do not bother me; the door is now shut, and my children are with me in bed; I cannot get up and give you anything'? I tell you, though he will not get up and give him anything because he is his friend, yet because of his importunity he will rise and give him whatever he needs.
>
> (Luke 11:5-8, RSV)

In this parable, Jesus outlines some of the essential principles of intercession. In his unique way, he doesn't give us a one-two-three guide, but provides a picture of prayer in the life of a person.

It is not likely that we will be too earnest in intercession if we do not have a keen sense of need. It may be, if we do believe in the power of intercessory prayer, that we will have to begin with ourselves—*praying that we will be sensitive to the urgent needs around us.*

REFLECTING AND RECORDING

To get a feeling for your level of sensitivity, survey concerns and needs of which you are aware.

1. List persons you know who are seriously ill _____.

_____, _____, _____.

2. Look at the community, town, or city in which you live. You do not have to be precise in your answers to the following questions:

What percentage of the people profess to be Christian? _____

What percentage of the people go to church on Sunday? _____

3. What are two of the greatest social needs; such as, poverty, alcoholism, juvenile crime?_____

4. Look at the church in which you are involved. On a scale of 1 to 10 (ten being the highest positive judgment) how would you rate the spiritual vitality of your congregation?

1   2   3   4   5   6   7   8   9   10

In quietness reflect upon the above information. Have you been praying for them? If not, how do you feel about your level of sensitivity?

Pray now, however you wish, including the above concerns. Close your time by praying the Lord's Prayer, keeping in mind the persons and concerns indicated in the above survey.

DURING THE DAY

If you had difficulty responding to any of the questions of the above survey, think about them today. Discuss the concerns with other persons who may have information and feelings about them which will be meaningful to you.

DAY THREE
Urgent Need

Yesterday we reflected upon the fact that we will not be too earnest in intercession unless we feel the urgency of concern. The survey was by no means exhaustive; only a minor mind-prodder to move us to deeper consideration of the needs around us.

If you have anything to add to the survey as a result of your thinking and conversation with others, do that now.

Let's prod ourselves a bit more. In the lefthand column list the first name of the first eight persons who come to your mind:

_____   _____

_____   _____

_____   _____

_____   _____

_____   _____

Go back now and think of each of these persons in terms of his/her needs. According to your knowledge, what is a deep concern of each of these people? Is any one of them physically ill? Is one lonely, struggling with a decision, wrestling with emotional anguish, experiencing mental depression, battling with a moral problem, caught in an unhealthy habit? Is any one of them not a Christian? Is one in need of food, shelter, clothing? Is one a child or teen-ager who feels separated from his/her parents or friends? Is one a teen-ager who is struggling for identity and expressing that struggle in unhealthy ways?

In the righthand column, opposite the written name, use two or three words to designate the needs of the person named. If you don't know enough about a particular person to name a need, leave it blank.

Now compare your list with the prayer list you have been keeping. Do you need to update your prayer list?

Read again the parable of the importunate friend from Luke 11, given on Day Two, page 73. Our Master's parable is so suggestive. The one who prays is asking for bread, *not for his own sake, but for his friend's.* He feels the poverty of his own life because of the need of another: "I have nothing to give him."

How that kind of praying is needed today! It is needed by parents who are insufficient in meeting their children's deepest needs. By teachers, physicians, and others who deal intimately with human life. By public servants and governmental officials who make crucial decisions daily. By friends who are committed to the well-being of one another.

REFLECTING AND RECORDING

With Jesus' parable of the friend at midnight in your mind, review the survey of yesterday and the names you listed today. Select two or three persons or concerns which will be central in your intercessory prayer for the remainder of this week. Do this by considering the degree of need, and the urgency you feel. Don't make this decision hastily. Mull over the survey and the list. Ask the Lord to give you direction in making your selections. Pray specifically for them.

Turn to page 155, and write your selections in the square marked "urgent." Then pray specifically for them.

DURING THE DAY

Clip this square to keep with you throughout the remaining days of this week. Let it remind you often to offer even "minute" prayers of "flash" prayers or love and concern.

DAY FOUR
Willing Love

On Days Two and Three of Week Two we concentrated on the love of God. We did not make the specific connection between my believing that God loves *me* and my practice of intercessory prayer. The connection is essential at two points. One, believing that God loves me affects the way I pray and the content of my praying. Two, believing that God really loves me is the bridge of understanding over which I walk to a belief that God loves others as well. Therefore, I can pray for others with confidence, knowing that God loves them as he loves me.

There is a crucial matter for us to face and overcome at this point. We tend to transfer distrust of ourselves to God. We know how difficult it is for us to love with no strings attached. So we transfer our limitation to God. That is why this is such an important matter. Though we may be limited in our capacity to love, God isn't. Before reading further, reflect on the thought that we transfer to God our inability to love with no strings attached, thus thinking he is limited in his loving. Write below any thoughts you have on this.

In the parable we are considering, the central character is a person of hospitality. Not only his home was a place of hospitality—the visitor felt he could knock on the door even at midnight—but also his heart was a place of hospitality. The weary, hungry traveler came at midnight and found a place of welcome.

The host did not excuse himself by saying he had no bread; he went out to seek it in the middle of the night. His night's rest and his own comfort were secondary to his friend's need.

Add to the feeling of *urgent need* the ingredient of *willing love,* and you have the dynamic of intercessory prayer. Here is a dramatic portrayal of that love in a word picture by Clarence McConkey.

> Ernestine is a deformed and ugly child. She drools at the mouth because she has no control over her swallowing. She is eight and weighs something like twenty-five pounds. She is fed through a tube which is inserted in her throat. She fouls her undergarments and is diapered like a baby. The neighbors cannot bear to look at her. The other children in the family are accustomed to her but do little for her because her parents have not wanted them to be burdened by her. Ernestine suffered cruel brain damage at birth, the doctors say. They also have said that with early treatment and therapy Ernestine might have been helped. She is now past helping, and the doctors advise the parents to have Ernestine placed in an institution.
>
> I think perhaps they are right, and yet I know her parents love her and I am not so sure that putting her in an institution is the thing to do. It is true that she would

get the medical care that she does not receive at home. Ernestine's parents are very poor and uneducated and unacquainted with many simple laws of health and hygiene. Yet every night of the week Ernestine's father comes home from work, chews food from the table, and forces it from his mouth into the tube and down the throat of Ernestine. This child lives on food chewed by her father. In an institution this would be done by a machine. It would be more sanitary and probably more effective.

But who is to say that it is not being done under expert care and supervision now? At least the doctors say Ernestine will never starve to death. Ernestine will die sometime before she is much older, I suspect, but in the meantime I have that image of a father in dirty jeans and T-shirt with grimy hands from work, holding a deformed child in his arms, hugging that child close to him, gently pushing the substance of life down a tube, holding and nourishing a frail bit of unlovely life which is made somehow lovely by his love. This is a picture that haunts me, a picture that taken in its entirety becomes a thing of almost ethereal beauty.[17]

It is the nature of love to give up—even to sacrifice and forget self for the sake of others. The New Testament word for this love is *agape*— unselfish, other-directed, with a feeling of active good-will, taking the needs of others and making them our own.

Love for others becomes in us the spirit of intercession. True love prays!

REFLECTING AND RECORDING

Look at your Urgent list from yesterday. Spend a few minutes thinking about how you love these persons, or if you are willing to love them in an agape fashion—unselfish, other-directed, with a feeling of active good-will, taking their needs and making them your own. This may lead you to specific prayer.

Here is a prayer by Thomas À Kempis. It throbs with the intensity of conviction of who God is and who we are in relation to him. As we make it our own, we yield ourselves to be searched and purified by the Spirit, and called to love.

Ah, Lord God, thou holy lover of my soul, when thou comest into my soul, all that is within me shall rejoice. Thou art my Glory and the exultation of my heart; thou art my Hope and Refuge in the day of trouble. Set me free from all evil passions, and heal my heart of all inordinate affections; that, being inwardly cured and thoroughly cleansed, I may be made fit to love, courageous to suffer, steady to persevere. Nothing is sweeter than Love, nothing more courageous, nothing fuller nor better in heaven and earth; because Love is born of God, and cannot rest but in God, above all created things. Let me love thee more than myself, nor love myself but for thee. Amen.

Pray the prayer over now. If you have difficulty with the words, write your own prayer here, using this model and thought.

DURING THE DAY

Go through the next twenty-four hours confident "that, being inwardly cured and thoroughly cleansed, I may be made fit to love, courageous to suffer, steady to persevere."

DAY FIVE
A Sense of Helplessness

Love is powerful. Compassion is a compelling force. Even so, though our compassion is deep and our love limitless, we may remain helpless in some situations.

The strongest love may be utterly impotent in a given situation. A mother and a father may be willing to give their lives for a dying child, yet be unable to save it.

As a pastor, so many times I have felt helpless as I have counseled with persons. Especially with alcoholics and the mentally ill, I have come to the point of despair, feeling that I had done everything, but had actually done nothing.

The fellow in Jesus' story was willing to give his friend bread, but he had none. It was his inability to provide what his friend needed that sent *him* begging. It is precisely this sense of helplessness, this impotence on our part, that is the very *strength* of our intercession.

"I have nothing to set before him." As this conciousness takes possession of us, we are, hopefully, driven to intercession. The sense of our helplessness becomes the soul of our intercession. Witness is piled upon witness, highlighting the redemptive power of intercession which flows from persons who know how limited, how utterly insufficient they are to meet the needs of those they love.

I'm thinking now of a couple in California. I was their pastor for five years. During that time and at least five previous years, the husband was almost completely prevented from functioning as a human being by alcoholism.

His wife tried everything—seemingly to no avail. She became a member of Al-Anon, a support group for spouses of alcoholics. She concluded that she was helpless. She continued to love him and began to pray earnestly for him. Two years after I moved from that community, I had a letter from her sharing the marvelous news that her husband had been sober for nine months. She had waited that long to write to test the reality of his transformation. This was seven years ago, and my friend is still sober. Neither husband nor wife would hesitate to affirm the role of prayer in his healing process. And he, especially, is quick to say that it is prayer—his and hers—that keeps him sober.

When we come to the point of helplessness, when we can say, "I have nothing to set before him," our intercession will possess that deep quality which is often called *supplication*. It is simply a feeling for, a wrestling with, and allowing the Holy Spirit to pray for us as he does. As Paul said, "Through our inarticulate groans the Spirit himself is pleading for us, and God who searches our inmost being knows what the Spirit means" (Rom. 8:26-27, NEB).

In our helplessness we are brought to the place where intercession is purified and becomes powerful. We come to the place of *utter faith in God to do what we cannot do.*

REFLECTING AND RECORDING

Is there a situation in your life about which you feel helpless? A need? A relationship? A person you really want to help, but seemingly cannot? Describe the situation here.

Sit quietly now with the situation you have described central in your mind. Hold that situation in your heart. Feel the intensity of it. Give it your love and concern. Don't rush, though you may be tempted to. Let all your feelings about it come forth. Stay with these feelings. Allow the Holy Spirit to search the depth of your innermost desires and pray for you.

DURING THE DAY

On Day One of this week we affirmed that Christian prayer is not telling God what to do; it is rather sharing our needs with him. Using occasions such as we have previously talked about—stops at traffic lights, waiting for appointments, etc.—continue to share with God in prayer today the need you have centered upon, about which you feel helpless. Throughout the day, as you pray, know that the Holy Spirit will pray within you as you pray.

DAY SIX
Importunity

> I tell you, though he will not get up and give him anything because he is his friend,
> yet because of his importunity he will rise and give him whatever he needs.
> (Luke 11:8, RSV)

Importunity. A strange word! We don't use it in normal conversation. It is somewhat archaic, but in this context I doubt if any other word would do. To *importune* means to press or urge or beg with troublesome persistence. A sense of urgency is always present when we *importune.*

This is obviously the central lesson of the parable. "Because of his importunity" the friend who went begging at midnight got what he needed.

Not only in our intercession, but in all our praying, we may not sense an immediate response. There may be delay—long delay. *Long, long delay!* It may even seem that God is saying, "I cannot give you what you ask."

We will come back to this point during this study because it is a common experience. The problem of "no answer," at least no apparent or immediate answer, is a plaguing one.

It is not easy, against all appearances of failure, to continue to pray—to hold fast, believing that God will hear and answer—to importune with the assurance that God will respond.

One key lesson of the parable is to be found precisely in learning what lies behind the importunity. Let's come directly to this rather than get tangled up in critical analysis of this parable to the point that we miss the big teachings. One of the most significant teachings is *our need for confidence in God.* There is no higher honor we can bestow upon God than to believe in him undauntingly, to have confidence that despite the agonizing delay or devastating silence or painful apparent refusal an answer will come! And the answer will be a blessing.

There is an effective dimension of importunity to which we give too little thought—*the accumulative effect of repetition in prayer.* This certainly applies to intercession.

When I am breaking up the soil to plant a garden, I plow it again and again in order to bring forth new soil from below the surface, to break up the clods, to loosen the earth to receive air and water.

In prayer, repetition is not simply duplication, but is an unfolding of the case. Our importunity—praying again and again—is not stale repetition, but the dynamic organ of novelty through which God allows us to see new facets of the need or new facets of our own experience.

After giving this dramatic picture of persistence, Jesus clinches his teaching about importunity. "I tell you, Ask, and it will be given you; seek, and you will find; knock, and it will be opened to you. For every one who asks receives, and he who seeks finds, and to him who knocks it will be opened" (Luke 11:9-10, RSV).

Importunity is an essential principle of prayer.

REFLECTING AND RECORDING

Recall a personal experience that you would label as importunity in prayer on your part. In a few sentences describe that experience enough to get it clearly in mind.

In the above experience were you praying for yourself or someone else? If for yourself, try to recall an experience of importuning for another. If for another, try to recall an experience in which your importunity was focused on your own need. Describe either briefly here.

Close your time by reflecting on the meaning of those experiences, and then pray for the persons or concerns on your urgent list, as well as your regular prayer list.

DURING THE DAY

Look at the list of persons you named on Day Three this week. Some of these persons are on your urgent list, some are not. Select one person to whom you will express love and concern today in a deliberate way, as a way of translating your praying into specific action. Decide now how you will express your love and concern.

DAY SEVEN
Shamelessness and Supplication

Yesterday we considered the dynamic quality of repetition in prayer. It is like reading the Bible. If the meaning of a passage does not come the first time, we read it again, and again—and again. Fresh meaning may come to a scripture passage we have read a dozen times before. This is certainly so as we read different translations.

The New English Bible renders Luke 11:8 thus: "I tell you that even if he will not provide for him out of friendship, the very shamelessness of the request will make him get up and give him all he needs."

There is a powerful suggestion of boldness here—*shamelessness.*

Imagine the harsh words from within coming to you, the beggar: "Shame! What nerve, waking me in the middle of the night. Let me alone. Get away. Go on home."

Our sense of helplessness makes us shameless in our seeking what we need. When our need is desperate, our prayers will move to that deep level we call *supplication*—an anguishing, feelings that may not have words, a wrestling from within. This is what Paul talks about in Romans: "In the same way the Spirit comes to the aid of our weakness. We do not even know how we ought to pray, but through our inarticulate groans the Spirit himself is pleading for us, and God who searches our inmost being knows what the Spirit means, because he pleads for God's own people in God's own way" (8:26-27, NEB).

The Bible has more than parables to confirm this dimension of shamelessness and supplication. It is a book of importunate and prevailing prayer. There is record after record of life struggles.

Jacob. No more would he be called Jacob, but *Israel* because of his all-night shameless supplication. He was to meet his brother Esau the next day. Jacob knew that he must have all night with God if he was to live. The sin of his youth had been found out. It took Jacob all night to see his sin as God saw it, and as Esau saw it. But he did see it. After that long night of shameless supplication, he called that place *Peniel,* saying, "For I have seen God face to face" (Genesis 32:30, RSV).

David. What midnight struggles he had with his sin! His couch was often wet with shameful tears. "Give ear to my prayer, O God; and hide not thyself from my supplication! . . . My heart is in anguish within me, the terrors of death have fallen upon me" (Psalm 55:1,4, RSV). Yes, at midnight—and more: "Evening and morning and at noon, I utter my complaint and moan, *and he will hear my voice*" [italics mine] (Psalm 55:17, RSV). Shamefulness led to shamelessness, and that to supplication.

Jesus. The mountains and olive groves of Galilee and Judea were places for his midnight shameless supplication. The bloody sweat of Gethsemane was real, climaxing a life of midnight knocking in shameless dependence upon the Father and in the bold confidence of the Father's love and response.

REFLECTING AND RECORDING

Go back to the experiences of importunity you recalled yesterday. Could you use the words *shameless* and *supplication* to describe your praying? Stop for a minute and think about that. Write your conclusion here.

Shift gears now. Do you know of any occasion in your life when someone prayed for you in *shameless supplication?* If so, briefly describe that experience here.

Pray specifically now, offering thanks to God for the witness of importuning prayer in the scripture, then make *shameless supplication* on behalf of the persons and concerns on your urgent list.

If you are in a group, your weekly meeting should be sometime today. Pray for those who will share with you in that meeting.

DURING THE DAY

If you were not able to express love and concern for the person you selected yesterday, seek to do so today.

If you identified someone who prayed for you in shameless supplication, find a way to thank that person today, perhaps by a telephone call, visit, or letter—and do it!

Remember the passage from Matthew 7:7-11 you clipped and began to carry with you on Day Four of Week One. Where is it? If you don't have the piece you clipped, review it on page 40 of your workbook, and take the promise with you into this day.

GROUP MEETING FOR WEEK FOUR

INTRODUCTION

One of our most significant experiences is praying *with* others. This is the way children, especially, learn the *value* and the *how* of prayer. It is not enough for our children or our friends to know that we pray. It is vital for them to pray *with* us, to hear us pray.

One big failure in much of our praying is our failure to be aware of and sensitive to what is happening as a result of our praying. This failure occurs at two levels. One, there are obvious answers to prayer that go unnoticed.

Two, we are so intent upon finding the dramatic answers that we often miss the subtle, deep changes of heart and mind taking place within us.

To live in friendship and fellowship with God, cooperating with his Spirit, living his life in the world—which is the goal of prayer—requires conscious effort on our part. A primary focus of this effort is the development of our sensitivity.

Not only praying with, but sharing with others is helpful in the development of our sensitivity. We need groups such as this to facilitate our sharing, but we also need to be intentional about sharing with persons who are not a part of our group. Many persons are inspired to pray by the witness of persons who are finding meaning in prayer. Our prayer experience is deepened and expanded as we think seriously enough about it to search out what meaning it actually has for us—*and to share that meaning with others.*

SHARING TOGETHER

1. Begin your sharing together by singing a hymn everyone knows.

2. Let each person share the most meaningful day of this week's workbook adventure.

3. Now share the most difficult day and tell why it was difficult.

4. Spend fifteen to twenty minutes, or more if necessary, allowing persons to share situations in which they practiced importunity in intercession for others, or some persons may share their experience of another offering ''shameless supplication'' for them. Ask participants to talk, especially about the *outcome* or *impact* of these experiences.

5. Allow persons to discuss any questions or concerns that have arisen during these four weeks. It is very important to verbalize our feelings and questions, and to have them received non-judgmentally by others. Share at the *intellectual* and *feeling* levels, but be very intentional about sensing the feelings of each other. Though some unanswerable questions may be raised, all should sense that at least their feelings are understood and accepted.

PRAYING TOGETHER

The Power of Touch

Most of us know the power of touch. A football player slaps the hand of a teammate. . . . A friend places an arm around our shoulder as we stand at the grave of a loved one. . . . A child throws arms around us for a joyous welcome home. . . . Our husband or wife quietly takes our hand and holds it warmly or touches it only fleetingly at a moment in a group when we need reassurance. . . . A handshake or a hug in parting is remembered long after words are forgotten.

Jesus took children on his knees to bless them. He often touched people to heal them. In prayer, also, the human touch is often important. We should not hesitate to hold a person's hand as we pray for him/her. It is a mystery, but somehow power—even the power of God—is transmitted person to person by touch.

Be aware in your group, and in your personal relationships, of the possible inherent power of the human touch. There may be occasions in your group, for instance, when you ask persons to place hands upon you as they pray for you. Miracles have come through groups gathering around a person, laying loving hands upon his/her head or shoulder, and "lifting" that person up in prayer.

1. By now persons in the group are probably willing to share much more openly and deeply than heretofore. Some will be willing to share questions and problems about prayer and intercession, as well as personal problems and concerns. As you begin your deliberate prayer time, ask for the sharing of any such needs. It may be a concern previously recorded on a 3 x 5 card will now be verbalized by the one who wrote it. After each sharing, allow time for one or two persons to pray aloud, as well as give time for all to pray silently, in response to the need. Don't forget the power of touch.

2. Corporate intercession is one of the great strengths of the Christian community. Who will ever know the power of the whole church joining in the Lord's Prayer, praying sincerely, "Thy kingdom come. Thy will be done"?

Last week you offered corporate prayers of thanksgiving for the church. In this session make corporate intercession for the church in the following fashion.

Let a person express a specific concern about the church, such as: "Lord give our pastor the wisdom and strength he needs to lead our congregation," "Heavenly Father, sustain Mary Brown in her missionary work as a nurse in Bogota," "Pour out your Holy Spirit upon us, O God, that we may be bold in our witness to those outside the church." After each specific expression of concern, the entire group will respond, *"You are hearing our prayer, Lord."*

3. Now have a corporate time of more general intercession. Let persons share any concerns. Persons and concerns that have been on individual prayer lists may be shared with the entire group at this time. Again the expression of need should be only in a sentence or two, followed by the response, *"You are hearing our prayer, O Lord."*

4. Sit in quiet prayer for two or three minutes, then the leader may simply say, "In Jesus' name. Amen," to close the meeting.

Keys for Effective Intercession 5

DAY ONE
Praying in Jesus' Name

One of the common maladies of Christians from Jesus' day until now is the debilitating willingness to be content without distinct answers to prayer. We pray daily (many of us), we ask many things, but living expectantly and knowing definite answers is too seldom a big part of our experience.

I have already confessed my reticence about being specific in my praying—especially in *tough* situations. As I examine my prayer pilgrimage, it is glaringly clear that for most of my life I have not claimed for myself the power that is available through the living Lord. The current growing edge of my life is precisely here—seeking to be constantly aware of the indwelling Christ, guiding and empowering.

Prayer is a primary channel of Christ's power into my life, and through my life into the lives of others.

The living Christ desires a daily relationship with us. From his perspective, a part of the result of that relationship is *answered prayer*. John records a number of Jesus' expressions of this.

> Whatever you ask in my name, I will do it, that the Father may be glorified in the Son.
>
> (John 14:13, RSV)

> If you ask anything in my name, I will do it.
>
> (John 14:14, RSV)

> You did not choose me, but I chose you and appointed you that you should go and bear fruit and that your fruit should abide; so that whatever you ask the Father in my name, he may give it to you.
>
> (John 15:16, RSV)

> In that day you will ask nothing of me. Truly, truly, I say to you, if you ask anything of the Father, he will give it to you in my name. Hitherto you have asked nothing in my name; ask, and you will receive, that your joy may be full.
>
> (John 16:23-24, RSV)

These words from the Gospel of John record repeatedly that the instruction of Jesus is that prayer be offered in his name.

That John repeated this bidding of Jesus over and over again and that this instruction was incorporated in the praying of the apostolic church give it a weight of meaning demanding our attention.

Unfortunately, ''in Jesus' name'' has become a rote closing to our prayers. We say it without thought, and so the meaning and power of it is lost to many of us. Obviously, these strong words of the Gospel have significance for faith. I believe they offer a key for effective prayer and intercession.

Some warnings may be in order. This is not a magic formula to guarantee our receiving what we ask in prayer. It is not to be thought that God is less willing to hear our prayers than Jesus, or that our prayers must be sponsored by Jesus in order to reach the Father's ears. Nor are we to think that in some magical way Jesus will give authority to prayers which might otherwise not obtain divine attention.

Having stated these disclaimers, the promise is still a bold one: All prayers offered in the name of Jesus are certainly received and answered by the Father.

How are we to understand such a bold assertion? Lewis Maclachlan says:

> Prayer in the name of Jesus is prayer that is offered not merely in our own right as individuals, but with authority derived from the fellowship of all believers in which we are members. ''We are no more strangers and foreigners, but fellow citizens with the saints in the household of God'' [Eph. 2:19]. It is this citizenship in heaven that gives us confidence. When we pray as Christians we are praying with the saints and indeed with the whole host of heaven. It is true that we need no further authority to come to God but that of our need and His love. Prayer, however, is not only a turning to God but a revolt from the powers of darkness. These we defy in the name of Christ against whom they did their worst in vain. When we pray in the name of Christ we assert the authority of one who has defeated evil.[18]

REFLECTING AND RECORDING

John Wesley once said, ''God does nothing but in answer to prayer.'' To be sure that is a bold overstatement. But it is dramatic enough to make us think. Jesus urged us to pray that God's kingdom power would prevail in every situation. The kingdom of God is indicated by Christ's ruling presence. That's what we pray for *in Jesus' name.*

Look at the major things you will be doing this day and the persons with whom you are involved. List them in these categories and time frames.

Time	What I'll be doing	Persons with whom I'll be involved
6 a.m.—Noon		
Noon—3 p.m.		
3—6 p.m.		
6 p.m.—12 midnight		
Midnight—6 a.m.		

Now move through your anticipated schedule and involvement, trying to imagine what it will mean for the Kingdom, "Christ's ruling presence," to pervade your day.

Here is a contemporary prayer by Jack W. Hayford. Read it and see if you can make it your own.

> Father, thank you for stretching me to become a responsible, maturing child of yours. I feel your longing to invade earth with your kingdom's love and power. Forgive me where I have doubted your readiness or almightiness to overrule the effects of sin.
>
> Mighty Lord, I embrace the truth which is freeing me from my sense of helplessness and bringing me to a sense of true authority in prayer. I ask you, Holy Spirit, to grant me boldness to withstand through prayer those destructive forces opposed to your loving plan. Believing the promise and privilege are mine, I accept the responsibility of prayer at this new dimension.
>
> Thine is the kingdom, the power and the glory. In Jesus' Name. Amen[19]

DURING THE DAY

Prayer in Jesus' name flows with power from lives lived *in Jesus' name.* Seek to express the Kingdom in your relationships and work today by intentionally giving yourself to the ruling presence of Jesus. Do this by being conscious that you are living and acting *in Jesus' name.*

DAY TWO
Praying in the Powerful Love of Jesus

We said yesterday that when we pray in the name of Jesus we are not merely praying in our own right or strength. We are praying as Jesus' disciples, as citizens of his kingdom, as members of his church. This means that our prayers can never be focused only on our private concerns. Prayer is an expansive concern with universal significance. This is a key to effective intercession. *In intercession we are united with the entire family of God because we are investing ourselves in the realization of God's reign throughout the universe.* Praying in the name of Jesus, we seek for ourselves, our loved ones, and others for whom we have special concern, the gift of God to all his children. So we press for further meaning to praying in the name of Jesus.

In the Bible *names* signify the meaning of character. Names of persons were believed to bear descriptive significance. To know a person's name was more than simply being able to address that person properly.

Praying in the name of Jesus, then, means praying in the powerful love of Jesus, because love was the supreme quality of his whole life. *Agape* is the Greek word for it, and we translate it into love. Jesus lived love, taught love, acted love. He *was* love. He and the Father are one in love, for God is love.

> To you whom I love I say, let us go on loving one another, for love comes from God. Every man who truly loves is God's son and has some knowledge of him. But the man who does not love cannot know him at all, for God is love.
>
> To us, the greatest demonstration of God's love for us has been his sending his only Son into the world to give us life through him. We see real love, not in the fact that we loved God, but that he loved us and sent his Son to make personal atonement for our sins. If God loved us as much as that, surely we, in our turn, should love one another!
>
> It is true that no human being has ever had a direct vision of God. Yet if we love one another God does actually live within us, and his love grows in us toward perfection. And, as I wrote above, the guarantee of our living in him and his living in us is the share of his own Spirit which he gives us.
>
> (1 John 4:7-13, Phillips)

We must not miss this, nor ignore it. To pray in the name of Jesus is to pray in love. The chief motive and the chief object of our prayers is love. Even the style of our praying, I believe, must reflect this.

I saw this reflected in Frank Laubach, probably the most impressive person I've ever met. His whole being, everything about him—the stance of his body, the expression on his face, the sound of his words—everything breathed love. Even when he prayed about the evils of war, he prayed for the enemy and he prayed in love, often with tears in his voice as well as in his eyes.

Again Lewis Machlachlan challenges us:

> If we cannot begin to pray in the spirit of love we must remain in prayer until our turbulent emotions are calmed by the consciousness of God, until all self-importance and self-pity subside, until that natural and good-natured indifference (which, and not hatred, is the worst enemy of love and the cause of so much

suffering in the world) is changed into a lively and active desire to share with all our neighbours the rich resources of our God.[20]

REFLECTING AND RECORDING

Spend two or three minutes reflecting on the claim that "natural and good-natured indifference . . . is the worst enemy of love and the cause of so much suffering in the world." Has indifference been a stumbling block to you? Write your thoughts here.

In light of your above conclusion, write a prayer expressing your feelings right now.

On Day Three of last week you made an urgent list. Look at that list and pray, in the powerful love of Jesus, for each person and concern.

DURING THE DAY

Today expand your practice of the instructions from yesterday.

DAY THREE
Cleansing Through Confession

> Come and hear, all you who fear God,
>   and I will tell what he has done for me.
> I cried aloud to him,
>   and he was extolled with my tongue.
> If I had cherished iniquity in my heart,
>   the Lord would not have listened.
> But truly God has listened;
>   he has given heed to the voice of my prayer.
>
> Blessed be God,
>   because he has not rejected my prayer
>   or removed his steadfast love from me!
>   (Psalm 66:16-20, RSV)

> If we confess our sins, he is faithful and just, and will forgive our sins and cleanse us from all unrighteousness.
>
>   (1 John 1:9, RSV)

Confession is at the heart of all prayer. Prayer is relationship with God, *communion.* Confession opens the door for communion.

The psalmist said, "If I had cherished iniquity in my heart, the Lord would not have listened." That is a strong word: "The Lord would not have listened." Note *listened.* God hears, yes! Because of who God is, supreme love and righteousness, our *communion* with God—God's listening and our honest speaking—is blocked if we *cherish iniquity in our hearts.* Sin is a barrier to communion; confession removes the barrier.

God is love, and to pray to God is to be in a communion (relationship) of love. Resentment, ill will, unforgiven acts and an unforgiving spirit, hatred, lust, selfishness—all such attitudes block our communion with God. Each of us could add to this list because it is by no means complete.

In intercession we seek to be channels through which our love and concern and God's love and power can flow into the lives of others. The channel must be kept as clear as possible. So confession is a cleansing, clearing process. The confession of our sins is a key to effective intercession.

One warning must be sounded. Don't strain to conjure up some shame or guilt that isn't there, in order to confess. Exaggerating or excusing any attitude or activity is not helpful. Simply be honest in confession, but also pray that the Lord will deliver you from self-deceit as you come to prayer.

REFLECTING AND RECORDING

There are generally five steps in the confession of sin, confession which cleanses us, making us clear and effective channels for intercession. Read them thoughtfully.

1. *Confession is first made to ourselves.* This calls for self-examination as we look at our lives, recognizing who we are, what we have done, what we are harboring in our lives that may block communion with God.

2. *Confession is then made to God, who alone can forgive.* It is important that we be deliberate in the first step so that we come to God not with general but specific confession.

3. *We accept God's forgiveness.* This is his grace, always given, but we must accept it.

4. *In the power of grace we renounce our sin.* We are cleansed and claim God's power to overcome our sin.

5. *We hold open our minds and hearts to God for his guidance which will assist us in redeeming or transforming the hurtful or evil results of our sin.* Frequently this involves confessing to and asking forgiveness of other persons we have wronged.

If you have these steps clearly in your mind, practice them by "praying through the steps" as you center upon the italicized phrases of each step.

DURING THE DAY

On Day Three of Week One you were given the word of Dr. Laubach: "Criticism of others nails them to the past. Prayer for them relases them into the future." As you go through this day, refrain from criticizing any person. When you are tempted to be critical, pray for the person instead.

DAY FOUR
Brokenness—A Channel for God

> O Lord, open thou my lips,
>   and my mouth shall show forth thy praise.
> For thou has no delight in sacrifice;
>   were I to give a burnt offering,
>   thou wouldst not be pleased.
> The sacrifice acceptable to God is
>   a broken spirit;
>   a broken and contrite heart, O
>   God, thou wilt not despise.
>   (Psalm 51:15-17, RSV)

One key to intercessory prayer is our own brokenness. I don't understand it. It is a part of the deep mystery with which we have to live and into which we have to enter. God responds to our brokenness.

God is all-powerful, but to give us freedom, to be full participants in our destiny and the Kingdom, God limits himself. God's power is operative in the context of human freedom and an orderly universe.

That is not a complete explanation of God's nature, but it is hoped it is enough to make my claim understandable. Because God has given us freedom, his love and care demand that in some instances he must *wait on us* to establish the conditions for him to do what he wants to do. My strong belief—based on experience and observation—is that often God has to *wait* until our spirits are broken and given to him to accomplish his work in us, and through us in others.

This seems to be a key to intercessory prayer. We are to worship God, to praise him, to give ourselves in obedience to him. In a day when worship centered around sacrifices offered to God, the psalmist dared to say:

> The sacrifice acceptable to God is
>   a broken spirit;
> a broken and contrite heart, O
>   God, thou wilt not despise.

Our brokenness may become the channel through which God's love and power flow into us, and through us into the life of another. We can somewhat better understand that if we have a personal relationship and contact with a person about whom we are concerned. But more mysterious is the fact that our prayers, emanating from "broken and contrite hearts," are effective on behalf of persons with whom we may have no personal contact.

Christian history is full of stories of revival and spiritual renewal taking place in communities when some person or group of persons became burdened for the spiritual condition of lost, suffering, unfulfilled persons. When that burden became a brokenness of spirit translated into committed intercession, somehow the Spirit of God was turned loose. God was able to do his work because of conditions established by the free response of persons.

REFLECTING AND RECORDING

"At the death of Robert McCheyne, the Scotch preacher, someone said, 'Perhaps the heaviest blow to his brethren, his people, and the land, is the loss of his intercession.' " [21] What an affirmation!

Spend a few minutes pondering this question: If you died who would suffer for the loss of your intercession?

Name three persons for whom you carry a burden of intercession.

_____

_____

_____

Is there a need within your church for which you should feel burdened? If so, write it here. If not, give thanks to God.

DURING THE DAY

Take one burden with you from this time of prayer. Call it to mind as often as possible today and let God work through your aching heart in relation to this need.

DAY FIVE
A Need for Boldness

As you begin this special time, spend a few minutes thinking about your daily life. Are you able to use the "during the day" suggestions? Are you trying? If not, why not? If you are trying, is it making a difference?

> And when they came to the crowd, a man came up to him and kneeling before him said, "Lord, have mercy on my son, for he is an epileptic and he suffers terribly; for often he falls into the fire, and often into the water. And I brought him to your disciples, and they could not heal him." And Jesus answered, "O faithless and perverse generation, how long am I to be with you? How long am I to bear with you? Bring him here to me." And Jesus rebuked him, and the demon came out of him, and the boy was cured instantly. Then the disciples came to Jesus privately and said, "Why could we not cast it out?" He said to them, "Because of your little faith. For truly, I say to you, if you have faith as a grain of mustard seed, you will say to this mountain, 'Move hence to yonder place,' and it will move; and nothing will be impossible to you."
> (Matthew 17:14-21,RSV)

I have already confessed my hesitancy to be precise in my pray-ing—hedging a bit that my faith will not be tested if the petition is not granted. At the heart of this hesitancy is a lack of *boldness.*

There are many reasons for this I am sure, not the least of which is my limited faith. I'm working on that. I've also discovered a more subtle, debilitating mind-set which hampers my prayer life and limits my boldness. I believe this is common to many persons as they become serious about prayer.

This debilitating mind-set is a false humility which makes a great virtue of self-depreciation. Don't leave this sentence too quickly because if you have fallen into this snare, the effectiveness of your praying is sorely limited. *A false humility which makes a great virtue of self-depreciation.*

Very early in my ministry, I was uniquely blessed by having a marvelous woman in my congregation. Because of her inspiration, encouragement, and prodding, I began to read and explore the broad expanse of prayer. She led a strong emphasis upon prayer in our congregation—prayer conferences, retreats, prayer groups, prayer chains. Because of the deep needs I felt as a pastor seeking to model a life of prayer and because of the people Mrs. Beeson knew through her long years of disciplined growth in prayer, I came in touch with some folk whom I saw as "giants in prayer," among them Louise Eggleston, E. Stanley Jones, Frank Laubach, Sister Lila, Tom Carruth, and Estelle Carver.

While I count those contacts and relationships as some of the most significant growth encounters of my life, I began to do a very stupid thing. I began to compare my prayer life to that of these "giants." Measuring myself by their stature I came out a midget. Thus came my false humility and my self-depreciation.

For many years, even now to too great an extent, I find myself tempted to cower in prayer, thinking, "Who am I to pretend such boldness in prayer."

But I am discovering something, and it is giving me boldness. We have to be careful to sort out false humility from authentic humility. When my humility is authentic, when I really see my weakness in its proper light, I can acknowledge my "nothingness" without self-depreciation. I do not apologize for my feebleness either in prayer or any other area of my life, but glory in that weakness, knowing that it is one of the conditions for receiving Christ's power. I remind myself of Christ's word that I need only faith—"faith no bigger even than a mustard seed" to move the mountains in my life and to share in the intercession that will move mountains in the lives of others and the world.

REFLECTING AND RECORDING

Look at your own life in light of my confession about self-depreciation. Has this been a problem with you? Are your feelings about yourself and your spiritual maturity limiting your boldness in prayer? Ponder these questions for a few minutes.

The following is a prayer expressing sweeping general concern. We need to be more specific in our praying, yet the expansiveness and boldness of this prayer by St. Clement of Rome is inspiring. Pray it as your own.

> We beseech Thee, Lord and Master, to be our help and succour. Save those who are in tribulation; have mercy on the lonely; lift up the fallen; show Thyself unto the needy; heal the ungodly, convert the wanderers of Thy people; feed the hungry; raise up the weak; comfort the faint-hearted. Let all the peoples know that Thou art God alone, and Jesus Christ is Thy Son, and we are Thy people and the sheep of Thy pasture; for the sake of Christ Jesus. Amen.

This is often the sort of general intercession we make in corporate worship. There is great meaning in such intercession, espcially if we give our minds and hearts to it with feeling and an effort at identification. Rather than sliding over the broad categories of need, we put "faces" in them.

Here are the categories of need in the prayer by St. Clement. Where possible, put some names with each category—persons you know or about whom you know. Write the names as an act of identification and boldness.

those in tribulation	the hungry
the lonely	the weak
the fallen	the fainthearted
the needy	the wanderers

Now, pray St. Clement's prayer again, holding names and faces in your mind as you offer each category of need.

DURING THE DAY

What is the most pressing problem you are facing today, or this week? Name it here.

_____

Pray boldly about this problem now. Then go through this day claiming, "There is nothing I cannot master with the help of the One who gives me strength" (Philippians 4:13, Phillips).

DAY SIX
Unselfishness in Prayer

By its very nature intercession is a commitment to the ultimate good of others. This is tough, especially as we pray for persons very close to us such as family members and intimate friends.

Recently one of my dearest friends was being interviewed for the presidency of a college in Nashville. It was an important career decision for him, and a crucial decision for the college. Nothing would have pleased our family more than to have these dear family friends live in our city. In the midst of that situation I found myself praying that my friend would be selected and would accept. I had moved from praying unselfishly for my friend, and for the best interest of the college. Unconsciously, *my* desires were pervading my praying.

One of the keys to effective intercession is unselfishness.

There is a dramatic story of unselfish intercession in the life of Moses. Israel has sinned blatantly against God. Moses knows it, acknowledges it, yet pleads for his people.

> On the morrow Moses said to the people, "You have sinned a great sin. And now I will go up to the Lord; perhaps I can make atonement for your sin." So Moses returned to the Lord and said, "Alas, this people have sinned a great sin; they have made for themselves gods of gold. But now, if thou wilt forgive their sin—and if not, blot me, I pray thee, out of thy book which thou hast written."
> (Exodus 32:30-32,RSV)

Moses is willing to give his own life in relation to God for his people. That is costly intercession. On Day Seven of Week Two we looked at Jesus as our prayer example. In his moving prayer in John 17, he prayed, *"For their sakes* I sanctify myself." Though the prayers of Jesus verbally reported in the Gospels are not many, his unselfish intercession is convincing. The unselfishness reached the ultimate height in Jesus' willingness to go to the cross on our behalf, and even there interceding for his enemies, "Father, forgive them; for they know not what they do."

Genuine intercession is unselfish. Our unselfishness is measured by the degree of our willingness to extend ourselves in love, at whatever cost, that our prayers may be answered. In my praying, as was the case as I prayed for my friend, I sometimes find that, without consciously doing so, I have designed an answer to my prayer. But unselfishness calls for a willingness to let go of our predetermined expectations of the answer, and a willingness to accept the answer which comes.

Harry Emerson Fosdick has given the clearest statement of why we do and don't pray.

> Before a man therefore blames his lack of intercession on intellectual perplexities, he well may ask whether, if all his questions were fully answered, he has the spirit that would pour itself out in vicarious praying. Is his heart really surcharged with pent devotion waiting to find vent in prayer as soon as the logic of intercession is made evident? Rather, it is highly probable that if his last interrogation point were laid low by a strong answer, he would intercede not one

whit more than he does now. *Intercession is the result of generous devotion, not of logical analysis.* When such devotion comes into the life of any man who vitally believes in God, like a rising stream in a dry river bed it lifts the obstacles at whose removal he has tugged in vain, and floats them off. The unselfish prayer of dominant desire clears its own channel. We put our *lives* into other people and into great causes; and our prayers follow after, voicing our love, with theory or without it. We lay hold on God's alliance for the sake of the folk we care for and the aims we serve. We do it because love *makes* us, and we continue it because the validity of our praying is proved in our experience. St. Anthony spoke to the point, *"We pray as much as we desire, and we desire as much as we love."*[22]

REFLECTING AND RECORDING

Examine your own life of prayer and your commitment to intercession in light of this judgment. Stay with this self-assessment for four or five minutes, then make your necessary confession and commitment to God. Write your confession and commitment here.

DURING THE DAY

Consider the involvements and activities that will demand large chunks of your time and energy today. Ask yourself, "Would the quality of my time and energy and the result of my involvement and activity change if I prayed for the persons with whom I share these involvements and activities?"
Let your answer determine your action in this regard.

DAY SEVEN
Confidence in Praying

Following the parable of the friend at midnight, Luke places some significant words of Jesus about prayer.

> And I tell you, Ask, and it will be given you; seek, and you will find; knock, and it will be opened to you. For every one who asks receives, and he who seeks finds, and to him who knocks it will be opened. What father among you, if his son asks

for a fish, will instead of a fish give him a serpent; or if he asks for an egg, will give him a scorpion? If you then, who are evil, know how to give good gifts to your children, how much more will the heavenly Father give the Holy Spirit to those who ask him!

(Luke 11:9-13, RSV)

The big word gleaned from these important words of Jesus is *confidence*. It is an essential principle of intercession. We begin our praying in confidence. We continue in confidence. We close our prayer in confidence. Even if we have to keep on praying, we do so, *confident* that the One to whom we pray is going to respond. If earthly parents know how to give good gifts to their children, how much more gracious, wise, and generous is our heavenly Father!

When *trust in God and love for men* co-exist in any life, prayer for others inevitably follows. Deepening intimacy with God, by itself, may find expression in quiet communion; enlarging love for men, alone, may utter itself in serviceable deeds; but these two cannot live *together* in the same life without sometimes combining in vicarious prayer. Now, such prayer has always been offered, not as a formal expression of well-wishing, but as a vital, creative contribution to God's good purposes for men. The genuine intercessors, who in costly praying have thrown their personal love alongside God's and have earnestly claimed blessings for their friends, have felt that they were not playing with a toy, but that they were somehow using the creative power of personality in opening ways for God to work his will. They have been convinced that their intercessions wrought consequences for their friends.[23]

We can pray with confidence. This confidence is rooted in our utter faith in *God's power and willingness to do what we cannot do*. Archbishop Richard C. Trench said, "We must not conceive prayer as an overcoming of God's reluctance, but a laying hold of his highest willingness."

REFLECTING AND RECORDING

Turn through the pages of this week's adventure, getting in mind the essential principles of intercession we have considered. Examine your own thoughts and experiences of intercession. Write here a paragraph describing where you are and what you feel and think about intercession. What principles have been missing? How do you feel about the possibility of incorporating these principles in your praying?

Pray for the persons and concerns on your urgent list.

If you are sharing this adventure with others, your group meeting is today. Pray by name for the participants. Pray that each person will be open to God and to others in the group.

DURING THE DAY

Keep the thought of Archbishop Trench with you throughout this day. "We must not think of prayer as an overcoming of God's reluctance, but a laying hold of his highest willingness."

GROUP MEETING FOR WEEK FIVE

INTRODUCTION

We pray because we must. We can't help it. It's a part of our nature. There is mystery here. We don't understand prayer. Just at a time when it seems a pattern is evolving and we have found "the secret," we are surprised. God can't be defined or put into a box. He works in his way, not ours, and on his time line, not ours.

It is a great day in our life when, without complete understanding or final explanation, we begin to practice prayer, especially intercession, in an intentional, committed way. We use whatever keys we find effective, but we should not allow ourselves to be too dependent upon "keys" or to get seduced into thinking that someday we will find an unbeatable formula. We hold in our mind the thought that prayer, like many of the profound experiences of life, often appears *absurd*. Lifetime commitment to another person in marriage, being overwhelmed by great music, being made speechless by the grandeur of some piece of nature's handiwork, crying at the mystery of birth or self-sacrificing love, moving to ecstatic joy or deep soul-searching in worship—such experiences, *along with prayer*, defy rational understanding or description. So we pray because we must!

SHARING TOGETHER

1. Let each person share which key to effective intercession he/she found most meaningful and tell why.

2. Spend a few minutes discussing and clarifying the claim of Maclachlan on Day Two that "natural and good-natured indifference" and not hatred is the worst enemy of love and the cause of so much suffering in the world. Ask the group to surface three examples.

3. Let the entire group review the five steps of confession considered on Day Three. Talk together about any or all these steps. What new insight came?

What step or steps do we most often leave out?

Which step is most difficult for each of us?

What does it really mean to perform step 4, "renounce sin" and claim power to overcome it?

4. Ask each person to share his/her thoughts about the question on Day Four: "If you died who would suffer for the loss of your intercession?"

5. Ask each person in the group to share his/her exciting thought or possibility about intercession as a result of this five-week adventure.

PRAYING TOGETHER

1. Begin your time of specific praying by thanksgiving. Let each person offer a sentence prayer, "Lord, I thank you for _____." Each person completes the prayer by naming something that is giving meaning and joy.

2. Now enter a time of *praise*. In *thanksgiving* we express our gratitude for something that has come to us, some gift from another or from God. *Praise* goes one step beyond *thanksgiving*. *We THANK God for what he has done; we PRAISE him for who he is*. The psalmist praised God in ways such as this: "Bless the Lord, O my soul; and all that is within me, bless his holy name!" (Psalm 103:1,RSV) Let persons offer their individual expressions of praise to God.

3. Confession is a key to all prayer and vital to intercession. Spend a couple of minutes in silent confession. Look again at the five steps on page 93 as you enter this brief period of silent confession.

4. Corporate confession is also important. Enter into a period of corporate confession, allowing as many as are led to offer a brief verbal prayer that will reflect a degree of corporate confession, such as, "Lord, we confess that we talk a lot about prayer, but pray very little."

5. Enter now into a period of corporate intercession, using the categories in the St. Clement prayer as given on Day Five. Read St. Clement's prayer on page 97. After each expression of concern, such as, "Save those who are in tribulation," stop and let individuals name persons they know with a descriptive word about that person's need. Allow enough time for as many persons to be named as the group may wish, then move on to the next expression of concern.

6. Allow any person in the group to share any need or concern he/she may have, with the group responding in prayer as you have been guided to do in one of the previous group prayer experiences.

Using Imagination And Practicing Nonverbal Prayer

DAY ONE
Relaxation and Receptivity

Through the previous weeks our emphasis has been primarily upon verbal prayer. This is the way most of us pray.

I believe in and practice verbal prayer. I speak aloud to God. I write down my feelings and thoughts.

I also listen to God. I listen to his words in scripture. I listen *within*, and in my imagination I sometimes hear God speak "verbally." I listen to other persons with sanctified imagination, believing that through them God often speaks.

The *listening within* verges on the nonverbal. It is nonverbal in that I don't hear sounds as I hear them when you address me in conversation. But it *is* verbal in the sense that in my imagination I hear God speak. I believe this is a crucial understanding.

On Day Five of Week Two, I shared that Father John Powell helped me get a mental hold on the different ports of entree God has to me—the ways God speaks other than through scripture, friends, and imagination. God speaks through my *mind*, giving me new ideas and new perspectives. God speaks through my *will*, giving me new desires or rekindling desires that have lost vitality, thus infusing me with his spirit and transfusing me with power. God speaks through my *emotions*, comforting me, calming me, troubling me, stirring me up, making me restless, healing me, or giving me peace. God speaks through my *memory*. When I need it, God stirs a stored-up memory to remind me of something he has done in the past relevant to my situation and need—an experience, a word, a relationship in which I was *with* God and I *heard, felt, and knew* God. Thus I am prevented from making mistakes. I am guided. I am renewed and strengthened through God's speaking to my memory.

We need to be aware, as we pray for others, that God can and does speak to them in many ways as well—certainly through *scripture, imagination, mind, will, emotion, memory, and other persons.* Believing this makes us more confident in our praying, but also introduces other possibilities than verbal prayer.

It is these other possibilities that we will consider and practice this week. Let's begin with a necessary element in this kind of praying: *relaxation as a key to receptivity.*

Many contemporary prayer leaders insist that relaxation, physical and mental, is a necessary step in praying effectively. The big idea is that we put ourselves into a receptive mood in order that we can receive what God has to offer. In prayer we make ourselves available to God so his resources can flow into and through us.

Jo Kimmel, in *Steps to Prayer Power*, provides a vivid image. "Have you ever had a garden hose which would get a kink in it, and even though you'd turned the faucet on full force, the water couldn't get through that kink? Well, that's often what happens to us; we've a kink, something which has made us tense and worried, and even though we anticipate God's coming to us and blessing us and flowing through us, he can't because of that kink. So, the very first thing we need to do in a time of prayer is to relax." [24]

By relaxing, disconnecting ourselves from the visible world and its problems, getting rid of our tensions, and freeing our minds of the clamor of competing thoughts, we may become more aware of God and thus more receptive to him; moreover, we may become increasingly more open channels through which his spirit may flow.

This is a good time to practice relaxation. Read the following directions carefully. Then read them a second time slowly, following the guidance. Give special attention to this exercise because we will build on it tomorrow.

Sit upright in your chair. Place your feet on the floor. Close your eyes. Let your full weight rest on the chair, no strain on your legs. Know the chair will support you. Keep your back straight, no slump, shoulders down and back. Breathe in deeply, long and deep. Now exhale completely, and as you do let your head come forward slowly until your chin rests on your chest. Now inhale deeply as you raise your head slowly, bringing it straight back as far as it will comfortably go. Now exhale, dropping your head slowly upon your chest.

Do this again, inhaling and exhaling with the movement of your head—slowly and regularly.

Now rest your head on your chest and breathe deeply, slowly, rhythmically three times.

Repeat the movement of your head to the rhythm of your breathing, but this time roll your head back over your right shoulder as you inhale and down over your left shoulder as you exhale. Then reverse the roll. Don't hurry. Repeat the roll and reverse the roll three times.

Let your jaws and neck completely relax. Feel the tension moving out of your shoulders. Yawn if you like. Let the feeling of inner quietness and calm pervade as you are physically relaxed.

Now lift your head to a comfortable position, keeping your eyes closed. Continue to breathe slowly and deeply, with the following affirmation of Psalm 46, set to the rhythm of your breathing:

God is my refuge and strength (inhale),

A very present help in trouble (exhale).

Repeat this breathing affirmation six or eight times. Then sit quietly for three or four minutes letting the awareness of the presence of God permeate your entire body.

REFLECTING AND RECORDING

Reflect upon your feelings about this relaxation exercise. Did you feel this was a prayer experience for you? Describe in a few sentences your awareness (or lack of it) of the presence of God.

Now as an act of praise and an affirmation of faith read aloud the following psalm:

O God, thou art my God, I seek thee,
my soul thirsts for thee;

my flesh faints for thee,
as in a dry and weary land where no water is.

So I have looked upon thee in the sanctuary,
beholding thy power and glory.

Because thy steadfast love is better than life,
my lips will praise thee.
So I will bless thee as long as I live;
I will lift up my hands and call on thy name.

My soul is feasted as with marrow and fat,
and my mouth praises thee with joyful lips,

when I think of thee upon my bed,
and meditate on thee in the watches of the night;

for thou hast been my help,
and in the shadow of thy wings I sing for joy.

My soul clings to thee;
thy right hand upholds me.
(Psalm 63:1-8,RSV)

DURING THE DAY

Select at least two occasions during the day to do the relaxation exercise and the rhythmic breathing affirmation:

God is my refuge and strength,
a very present help in trouble.

Record here your selected time to practice relaxation.

_____

_____

DAY TWO
The Prayer of Loving Regard

Begin your reflection and prayer time today by praising God with Psalm 24 as paraphrased by Leslie Brandt. In this psalm there are three great lessons:

> One, everything belongs to God, and we owe God our allegiance.
> Two, as we seek to do God's will, we discover God's true purposes for our lives.
> Three, within God's will we can overcome our personal anxieties and give ourselves unselfishly for others.

These lessons flavor our praying.

> Let us never forget that this world
>   and everything in it belongs to God.
> But not all of this world's citizens
>   recognize or give allegiance to their Creator.
> Who are they who truly love and serve God?
> It is they who discover and live
>   within His purposes for their lives.
> It is they whose hearts and hands
>   are dedicated to His will for them.
> It is they who turn away
>   from self-centered concerns
>   to live for others about them.
> They are the ones who can count
>   on God's perpetual blessings.
> They nevermore need to be concerned
>   about their personal salvation.
> They have been delivered from such anxiety
>   to focus their effort and endeavors
>   on communicating God's eternal love
>   to their fellowmen.[25]

Be quiet for two or three minutes and let the message of the psalm sink in.

Most of us who have thought of prayer primarily as thoughtful verbal activity may think that meditation and an emphaisis on the intuitive feeling dimension of prayer are recent developments. Not so. In many of the classic descriptions of prayer the ultimate was "the prayer of deep quiet."

Many "spiritual athletes" have tried to climb "the ladder of perfection" in prayer. The lowest rung was known as *oral prayer* and many looked down upon this form of praying. I suppose they forgot that Jesus taught oral prayer, and was not beyond crying aloud on the cross the deepest prayer of his heart.

The second rung was termed *mental prayer* and the emphasis was upon thinking. In the West we associated this form of prayer with meditation. Until recently, however, meditation was neglected. Even our "quiet time" has been usually spent praying silently, but *verbally*, rather than meditating.

The third rung was *affective prayer*, or "the prayer of the heart." The stress here was on feeling.

The top rung was the prayer of *loving regard* or "deep quiet," which involved not just words and feelings but our whole being. In this prayer of loving regard the effort was to be with God—loving, adoring, praising him. In the mystical tradition of the church the goal was union with God. Unfortunately this effort expressed itself in somewhat bizarre ways as persons sought to submerge themselves into God. I am not condemning the mystical tradition, only some extreme expressions of it.

The idea in its wholeness is valid. We need, however, to think of *communion* not *union*. The purpose of prayer is being *with* God, not *losing ourselves in God*. God's action in our lives doesn't abolish the self, but uses the whole self.

Yesterday, in the relaxation prayer exercise, we began to practice what may be a combination of *affective prayer* and *the prayer of loving regard*. This kind of praying can be used in intercession. We bring our whole being—body, mind, and heart—into the presence of God *in loving regard*. We do this by relaxing, becoming quiet, freeing ourselves of mental and physical tension, and centering ourselves attentively in God's presence. Then we bring into that *loving regard* a vision of the person for whom we wish to pray.

Think now of a person for whom you wish to pray. Write that person's name here: _____.

If you know the person, get a picture of him/her clearly in mind, the person's need, and what you think God may wish for that person. You may write that need here:

Now use the relaxation exercise suggested yesterday. When you get to the rhythmic breathing affirmation use these words:

I breathe the love of God within (inhale);
and give my life in love to him (exhale).

Repeat this breathing affirmation six or eight times, giving yourself in loving regard to God—body, mind, and heart. Then bring into that loving regard a vision of the person you designated above, using this breathing affirmation:

I breathe the love of God within (inhale),

and I send that love to _____[name of person] (exhale).

Repeat the affirmation six or eight times while naming the person. Then sit in silence with feelings of love for God and love for the person for whom you are praying radiating out to that person. Don't hurry, for love brings healing.

REFLECTING AND RECORDING

Let this experience stand. Don't try to analyze it or test it. Simply affirm it by offering praise to God, and end by repeating the psalm with which you began.

DURING THE DAY

Twice in this adventure you were given the word of Frank Laubach, "Criticism of others nails them to the past. Prayer for them releases them into the future." As you go today, change your criticism into prayer.

One of the suggestions for your prayer time tomorrow is to tape-record the meditation. If that is a possibility for you, find some time later today to do it so that you will be ready to receive full value from the exercise tomorrow.

DAY THREE
The Healing at the Pool

Carolyn Stahl's book, *Opening to God*, is a marvelous resource for guided imagery meditation on scripture. This form of praying makes powerful use of imagination and meditation. By meditation I mean both the deliberate, mental reflection into which we consciously enter and the more intuitive flow of imagination, images, feelings, and thoughts which are spontaneous rather than controlled or deliberately called forth rationally. God is immediately present in the depths or heights of our being. The meditative form of prayer seeks to free or release the expression of the Divine within us. Today let's use one of Dr. Stahl's meditations as a resource for this form of praying.

When you get to the guided meditation on the *Healing at the Pool* printed below, you may do the meditation in one of three ways. (1) Alternate reading and closing your eyes in order to visualize it. (2) Read the whole meditation several times, then visualize it as you remember it, without worrying whether you include every detail. (3) Tape-record the meditation in advance with slow quiet voice, then listen to the guided meditation at the appropriate time.

First, get the scripture in mind, for it is the basis of your guided imagery meditation.

> Now there is in Jerusalem by the Sheep Gate a pool, in Hebrew called Bethzatha, which has five porticoes. In these lay a multitude of invalids, blind, lame, paralyzed. One man was there, who had been ill for thirty-eight years. When Jesus saw him and knew that he had been lying there a long time, he said to him, "Do you want to be healed?" The sick man answered him, "Sir, I have no man to put me into the pool when the water is troubled, and while I am going another steps down before me." Jesus said to him, "Rise, take up your pallet, and walk." And at once the man was healed, and he took up his pallet and walked.
>
> (John 5:2-9,RSV)

Think of some particular part of your body in which you would like to have greater health. Or if you would like to think of this emotionally, intellectually, or spiritually, think of some aspect of your life which you would like to have made more whole. Close your eyes:

Guided Meditation

> Sit quietly and take a few slow, deep breaths. . . . Allow the tension in your body to be released. . . . Imagine yourself by a pool of water. . . . Notice what people are with you as you are beside this pool. . . . Notice what the edge of the pool is like. . . . Look at the water and notice the color, the temperature, the texture. . . . Notice the details of this pool. . . . Now become aware of your own body and of a particular area which you would like to be more healthy. . . . Observe the Christ walking toward you, sitting down beside you, and asking you what you are doing. You respond, telling the Christ why you are there. . . . Christ asks you if you want to be made whole. . . . Feel free to interact. Communicate in any way that feels right for you. . . . Decide with the Christ what you are going to do. . . . You may simply get up, affirm your wholeness, and walk on home. Or, you may move into the water and swim around, splashing, and feeling the wholeness cleansing and healing your body. Or, you may come to understand some guidance. . . . Let yourself finish this scene as feels right for you. Stay in touch with the quality of health and wholeness that surrounds the water in this pool, the faith and conviction that you and Christ share. . . . Know that you can return to this setting in your imagination whenever you want. . . . When you are ready, open your eyes.[26]

REFLECTING AND RECORDING

It would be naive to think that a one-time meditation like this would adequately introduce you to the techniques and tools for guided imagery meditation. This is an introduction which hopefully you will use in the future. It is important for you to record what you have experienced in this meditation. Write your reflections here. Be honest.

How did it go?

What did you feel?

What insights came?

What seemed irrelevant?

Note: Further meaning may come later. If so, return and record that insight here.

DURING THE DAY

While I believe in instant healing, the norm seems to be that healing comes gradually. This is true in physical, emotional, and spiritual healing. Cultivating awareness of the living Christ is a dynamic part of that healing process. In the guided meditation, you were told that you could, in imagination, return to the setting of the pool of healing whenever you wished. Do that deliberately at least twice in the next twenty-four hours.

Tomorrow you will have the opportunity to use a guided meditation as intercession for another. If you wish to tape-record the meditation find a time to do so today. Otherwise choose one of the other two ways suggested.

DAY FOUR
Bringing Another to the Pool of Healing

Yesterday the guided meditation focused on you. Today practice the same kind of meditation as an intercession for another. Get in mind a person who needs healing—physical, emotional, spiritual. In the guided meditation this person will be referred to as your friend.

Turn back to yesterday's exercise and read John 5:2-9. Affirm your belief in the healing power of Christ, then do the following meditation. If you are physically weary or tense, do the relaxation exercise suggested on Day One of this week.

Guided Meditation

Take a few slow, deep breaths. Close your eyes, relax, and let tensions leave your body. Imagine yourself with your friend on a hillside . . . there are few trees . . . and not much grass. You are on a dusty, well-worn path. There are other people around, but you don't pay them much attention. In the distance, on another hill, you see some colonnades glistening in the sun. You know a pool is there, and you are headed for it. You have heard that the water of that pool has a healing quality. You are taking your friend there. The two of you move down the path. It is hot and dusty, but you are excited. Notice whether you are walking fast or slowly as you get closer to the pool. Notice if there are other people. Experience how you feel as you approach.

You pass through a colonnade and see the pool, glistening in the sun . . . cool . . . refreshing. Look at the sparkling water . . . the color . . . your shadow dancing in it. . . . You and your friend stand beside the pool . . . waiting . . . you are not sure for what. There's something about the water. You feel like you may want to get into the water. There's a pull toward it.

Now you become aware of a person standing with you. You recognize Jesus. You feel that he knows you, but you introduce yourself and your friend to him. The three of you sit down beside the pool and begin to communicate. How do you feel with Jesus? Let Jesus respond. He asks you why you are there. Tell him about your friend's need for healing. . . . Feel the love flowing from Jesus' eyes as he asks your friend, "Do you want to be whole?" . . . Your friend begins to talk. You are still and quiet as the two begin to share . . . you can feel Jesus' tenderness. Notice your friend's face . . . the expression . . . the light in your friend's eyes . . . you know something is happening . . . your friend is receiving Christ's healing love. You are there . . . you see Christ and your friend . . . yet you are not a part of the conversation now . . . you know something beautiful and good is happening to your friend . . . so you wait.

Now Jesus responds to you . . . you know it is right for you to enter the conversation again. So finish the conversation as it feels right for you and your friend. You know that Jesus will have to leave and so do you. So you say goodbye in a way that is comfortable for you. . . .

Stay aware of the quality of health and wholeness that surrounds the water in the pool, the faith you and Jesus share and now your friend shares. Know that you can return to this setting in your imagination whenever you want. . . .

When you are ready, open your eyes and sit quietly for as long as you wish.

REFLECTING AND RECORDING

Sit quietly, and continue to hold lovingly in your mind a picture of your friend, and reflect upon what happened in your meditation. Record your reflections here: feelings, questions, thoughts that came into your mind that didn't seem to fit the meditation, bits of conversation or significant words that you may have heard Jesus or your friend speak. Write enough to capture your feelings and thoughts about the meditation.

On Day Six of Week Three you were asked to be especially attentive to whether an avenue for action, involvement, or relationship had opened for you as you prayed for someone or some concern for which it seemed impossible to act. Check that out now and describe what happened.

DURING THE DAY

Carry with you into the day a picture of your friend's talking with Jesus by the pool. Every time you see water today remember your meditation;

though it may be for a very brief time, get a clear picture in your mind of your friend and Jesus by the pool.

Tomorrow there will be another guided meditation, so if you wish to tape-record it, find some time today to do so.

DAY FIVE
Let God Speak to and Through Your Imagination

Robert Keck describes four types, or categories, of meditative prayer. They are not mutually exclusive, nor do we need to use them separately. Yet, they do provide a well-rounded approach to Christian prayer. The four types are: (1) communion with God simply because God is God; (2) communion with God for full self-actualization, to realize our own potential for wholeness; (3) communion with God in our linkage with others; and (4) communion with God in order to listen.[27]

The third type is a form of intercession and is based on the conviction that all of us, in the very depths of our being, are linked, interrelated. Research is confirming this linkage rather convincingly. Talking about his research with fellow physicist Harold Puthoff at the prestigious Stanford Research Institute, Dr. Russell Targ said, "We are proving unequivocally that there is a paranormal channel of human communication. We don't know how it works, but it works reliably and independent of distances."[28] Dr. Targ is saying that there can be communication (such as mental telepathy) among humans other than through what we think of as normal channels.

Meditative prayer is such a channel. It provides the channel through which we can send love, light, and health-giving energy to others. Likewise we can receive the same from others who pray for us. This underscores one of the principles involved in the meditations we have been using this week. This kind of communication is most effective when we are in a deepened state of consciousness, and are giving freedom to the intuitive, imaginative capacities of our brains. Thus we become silent and seek to move into a very relaxed state. Do this now. You may want to use the relaxation exercise you used on Day One of this week.

In the following meditation let God speak *to* you and *through* you to another.

Close your eyes. Imagine yourself walking along a secluded beach. The sun is warm, but not uncomfortably hot. How do you feel about being on the beach—the rest and peace you are enjoying? You have with you either a blanket or a beach

Note: Carolyn Stahl's *Opening to God* (The Upper Room, 1977) and Robert Keck's *The Spirit of Synergy: God's Power and You* (Abingdon, 1978) are excellent books for individual and group use for those wishing to pursue guided imagery and imagination in prayer and to practice meditative prayer.

chair—whichever is more comfortable for you. Look around you. Find a place where you will be most comfortable. Fix your blanket or chair and settle down to enjoy the beauty of the setting.

Feel yourself a part of the scene . . . the warm sun on your face . . . the gentle breeze . . . the fine texture of the white sand. Be aware of the clear blue sky . . . fluffy white billowy clouds here and there . . . the spray of the waves hitting the rocks . . . sea gulls soaring gracefully on the air in the wind. Hear the cawing of the gulls . . . the splash of the waves on the rocks . . . the gentle return of the waves on the sand.

It's beautiful . . . relaxing . . . peaceful . . . comfortable. Be aware that you are a part of it . . . become one with it. God has created you and all that surrounds you. You are interlinked with nature, interlinked with God. All are parts of one another. Rest now in the peace of this setting and in the peace of God permeating your whole being. Think of the warm sun on your face and body as the warmth of God's love and light shines upon you. The gentle breeze is his spirit. Bask in this awareness. You feel a quiet joy, peace . . . all is well.

Your silence is broken not by a sound, but by a friendly presence. A person is walking toward you. Who? Do you recognize the person? Whoever this is, you know this one is special. Invite this special friend to sit with you. Share what you are experiencing there on the beach . . . then let the conversation flow, however it will. . . . Don't hurry . . . just be together with your guest sharing this beautiful place . . . experience it together.

Let your friend talk . . . you talk to your friend. Your friend will let you know when it's time to part. At that time you may stay as long as you wish, absorbing the warmth and beauty and peace of the beach. Then take a deep breath, open your eyes, and return to your own place.

REFLECTING AND RECORDING

Our imagination is a great channel through which God comes to us and to others. Spend some time thinking about the person you met on the beach and the significance of that particular person being the one who came to you. This may be easier if you recognized the person. If you didn't, think about who the person is, or what the unknown one may represent. Sometimes the image is not clear but may become clear in the future. Describe your experience here.

DURING THE DAY

Allan A. Hunter has provided us a good image that we can carry with us today from our deliberate time of prayer. He suggests that we think of ourselves as little rods of steel in a magnetic field. In our time alone with God we become magnetized.

> This means that for the rest of the day we should be enabled to point more or less straight toward the Magnetic Pole, that unlimited Caring we see in Jesus that enables us to be honest. To be sure, there will be waverings, distractions and so on, but again and again the power within us, the Holy Spirit, will bring us back to where we belong. In that Power we now relax, hoping for more silence of the will as well as mind. After the "So-be-it-Amen!" we exhale a wholehearted "Thank!" and inhale a grateful "You!" and up we get.
>
> So that throughout the day we will be more open and responsive to the Presence that would guide and strengthen us, we can offer up when appropriate and if we are reminded, one or other of these "outreachings," "overflowings of the heart", "arrow-swift prayers", or "flash mantras":
>
> (When about to meet someone), "Won't You, O God, express at least a little of Your interest in this person through me right now?"
>
> (Standing before a flower garden, the setting sun lighting up the sky with color or a child laughing), "I breathe Your shining beauty in/To call forth the creative asleep in me."
>
> (Before opening the hospital door into the room where a patient is worried about next day's operation): "You, O God, are in charge. I trust You to show me what to do or say or what not to do or say."
>
> (Facing a difficult assignment where much is at stake), "In You I Can!"
>
> The openness which comes from a discipline such as we have been considering, does bring harmony and meaning to the day so that at the end we can feel it has been "stitched together;" that is, if we stay with it.[29]

DAY SIX
Conversation in the Presence of Christ

Begin your time today with a few minutes of praise by reading this psalm, as paraphrased by Leslie Brandt:

> It's a glorious feeling to be able
>   to unload my heart,
>   to spill out my gratitude
>   in thanks to You, O God.
> Morning, noon, and night
>   I want the whole world to know of Your love.

6

I want to shout it, to sing it,
   in every possible way
      to proclaim Your praises,
         to express my joy.

How great You are, O Lord!
Your thoughts are unfathomable,
   Your ways beyond comprehension.
And all the while we are still confounded
   over the problem of evil.
We simply cannot understand
   why the ungodly appear to be so successful,
   why good fortune seems to follow those
      who defy You.
But we know their success is short-lived.
Those who refuse to turn to You will never find
   that ultimate and total fulfillment
      that is promised to the sons of God.

The children of God,
   those who open their lives to You,
      portray the wonder and beauty of Your Spirit.
They are like springs of water in a parched world.
They flourish even amid the distortions
   and the ugliness around them.
Their lives are rich and productive
   in a barren and desolate society.

Help us, those of us who love You, O God,
   to prove to our disjointed world
      that You are in our midst.[30]
        (Psalm 92)

Remain silent for two or three minutes, praising God in your heart.

Joe Harding, a friend of mine, taught me something about prayer that I have expanded and found meaningful in a number of ways. I was having difficulty with a colleague. There was tension between us. I felt he did not trust me. There was a lack of freedom in our relationship, no spontaneity. He seemed to keep me at arm's length. He was seemingly unable to affirm any idea that came from me.

I was deeply concerned, and often prayed for this person and our relationship. But nothing positive seemed to happen. I shared this with Joe, and he suggested that I pray for my friend by having, in my imagination, a conversation with him in the presence of Christ. The process was that I would speak to my friend and imagine my friend's response. I had to be honest in the expression of my feelings, and equally honest in imagining my friend's words to me. I was to receive my friend's words as though they were actually his.

Imagining Jesus present with us deepened the exchange, inspired honesty and depth of feeling—also acceptance of each other.

I tried it for a number of days. After four or five deliberate experiences, two things began to happen. I began to see my friend in a different light. I began to sense the fear and pain of his life, his insecurity. My apparent security threatened him. Secondly, a new openness developed. We became freer with each other.

This gave me a clue for a form of prayer which uses the imagination for visualization. One of the primary ways I use it now is by having a three-way conversation among whomever I wish to pray for, Jesus, and myself. I use it a lot when I drive. I use it also to pray for people about whom I'm concerned but about whom I know little and who are removed geographically from me. I simply visualize the three of us—Jesus, the other person, and myself —driving down the highway together, or in some quiet place, having a conversation. I simply talk to Jesus about the person with that person present in my imagination.

This kind of praying helps me hold a person in love in the presence of Christ, and enables Christ to direct me in my relationship to the person. I am convinced from experience that Christ speaks through our imagination as much as in any other way. I am equally convinced that, in some mysterious way that we may never understand, what happens with us and Christ in our imagination has influence on others.

REFLECTING AND RECORDING

Select a person with whom you may have had difficulty relating, and have a conversation with that person in the presence of Christ, as I did with my friend. Or if you can't identify such a person, select someone about whom you are concerned and have a conversation with that person and Jesus.

Spend at least four or five minutes in this conversation. Then write here your feelings about it. Don't hesitate to share your difficulties if you have any.

DURING THE DAY

Experiment with this form of prayer as conversation in the presence of Jesus. You can do it almost anywhere when you are alone, or where there are not too many distractions.

DAY SEVEN
Visualization Prayer

Begin your prayer period with praise to God. Read the following psalm paraphrase, then sit in silence for two or three minutes praising God in your heart.

O God,
   in the grace and strength that You daily grant,
      Your servant finds reason for celebration.
You have truly fulfilled his innermost longings.
You have responded to his deepest needs.
He asked for security,
   and You encompassed him with love.
He looked to You for life,
   and You granted him life eternal.
He sought for identity,
   and You adopted him as Your son.
Whatever is of value and worth in his life
   has come by way of Your rich blessings.
His heart is glad in the realization
   of Your eternal presence.
He knows that he will never lose Your love.
   I raise my voice in praise, O God,
   because no one can separate me from You.
Though circumstances threaten me
   and my own obsessions entangle me,
      You will never let me go.
Your great power is sufficient to set me free
   from these things that hurt my soul.
If I put my trust in You,
   You will not allow them to destroy me.
I find so many reasons for praising You, O God.[31]

                    (Psalm 21)

The big idea in the form of praying we have used this week is that we are to give God an opportunity to speak through and work through a dimension of our being—the intuitive, imaginative, nonverbal—which we have glaringly neglected, especially in the western world. The Bible offers many illustrations of God's speaking and working in this fashion. Dreams, visions, images are a common part of the biblical witness. Jesus talked about the "kingdom within." It is necessary, then, to give attention to the within-ness of God. This is one of the primary facets of the Christian faith—that God dwells in us through the Holy Spirit, and this Holy Spirit is the dynamic expression of the living Christ.

In meditation we, as Christians, seek to cultivate an awareness of God within, whom we know as the living Christ. We do not limit our prayer life to the verbal, rational, logical mode of consciousness. Rather, we avail ourselves of Divine communion and guidance which come through the intuitive, imaginative, creative mode. We know that the mind includes such functions as reason, will, intuition, imagination, and emotions, so we seek to be open to God in developing, balancing, and integrating these various functions.

In her book *Steps to Prayer Power,* Jo Kimmel suggests a number of effective ways to practice another form of imaginative and nonverbal prayer. She calls it *visualization.* Read these two visualizations, before you try to practice either.

If there's someone you resent or hate or feel contempt for, sit quietly, relax, rest, wait, then visualize Jesus standing in front of you, looking at you with compassion and understanding and tell him how you feel about the person. Tell him you know this feeling keeps you from receiving all the good you can from him. Ask him to melt your heart with his love. Then visualize your heart being melted by his love and that love flowing out from you. See the stream of love flowing to the person you've let come between you and God. Just let it flow for a while and then end your visualization prayer with gratitude for your imagination and for what Jesus has done in melting your heart and letting love flow through you.

It may be there's more than one person you've been separated from, and this would be a good time to see the love flowing to others who have hurt you or misunderstood you and whom you've misunderstood. Take your time with each one. Keep your breathing deep and regular and your body relaxed. Never hurry this process, rather let it flow slowly from you.

First, of course, relax, breathe deeply and regularly, and grow quiet inside. Take your time to do this. Then imagine a ray of light shining down on you. It's a ray of white light and feels warm and comfortable to you as it shines on you. Rest in the relaxing warmth of it and feel it penetrating into every cell of your body, until you're aglow with the light. Picture it radiating from you, forming a pool of light in front of you. It is deep and clear. When the image is strong—and take time to see it and enjoy it—bring someone you want to pray for to the pool. See him walk into it or jump into or dive into it. Somehow, as you do this particular experiment, the persons you bring to the pool take on a life of their own as they walk with you to the pool, and you'll often find that they'll enter the pool in unexpected ways. Let them, and watch as they eventually become submerged in the pool of light. Then you're ready to bring another and watch him or her, then another, and another, never hurrying the images or leaving out some of the steps, but taking time to see the action of the scene unfold before your inner eyes.

When you've brought all the persons to the pool that you want to bring, then bring your church, the minister and congregation, bring your city, your state, your nation, and the world. End your experiment with words such as these: "Thanks so much, Father, that I could bring these people and situations to you. Thank you that your healing light is meeting the needs in each one. Thanks." [32]

REFLECTING AND RECORDING

Select one of the above ways for visualization prayer and practice it now.

DURING THE DAY

Go back and review the instruction for During the Day on Day Five of this week. Practice that kind of praying throughout this day.

GROUP MEETING FOR WEEK SIX

SHARING TOGETHER

There may be a lot of questions to be shared and discussed about this week's experience. This is as it should be, since the style of praying used this week may be new for several within the group. Try to stay away from questions about the method until some personal experiences have been shared.

1. Let each person share an experience of meditative prayer that was especially meaningful. Take enough time for persons to share some details of the experience.

2. Now talk about the difficulties you may have had actually praying in this fashion. Please be careful not to discount the validity of this approach to prayer without allowing time to experiment with it.

3. Spend a little time sharing questions, but don't get hung up here since what we have done this week is only an introduction. You may want to talk about the possibility of someone's ordering Stahl's and Keck's books for persons to read following this adventure. You may want to continue your group meeting for a few weeks after you have finished the workbook, using Stahl's book as a source of guided imagery meditation.

4. Spend the balance of your allotted time for sharing (save at least fifteen to twenty minutes specifically for prayer) talking about your feelings about the group's disbanding after next week. If you wish to continue as a group, what will your format be? What will you study?

PRAYING TOGETHER

1. The following is a guided meditation by Carolyn Stahl. The leader will direct the entire group in this meditation. The focus is not intercession but will be practice in guided imagery meditation for a *group*. Be sure that everyone is in a comfortable position, sitting very upright and relaxed. The leader reads:

> On another occasion he began to teach by the lakeside. The crowd that gathered round him was so large that he had to get into a boat on the lake, and there he sat, with the whole crowd on the beach right down to the water's edge. And he taught them many things by parables.
>
> As he taught he said:
>
> "Listen! A sower went out to sow. And it happened that as he sowed, some seed fell along the footpath; and the birds came and ate it up. Some seed fell on rocky ground, where it had little soil, and it sprouted quickly because it had no depth of earth; but when the sun rose the young corn was scorched, and as it had no root it withered away. Some seed fell among thistles; and the thistles shot up and choked the corn, and it yielded no crop. And some of the seed fell into good soil, where it came up and grew, and bore fruit; and the yield was thirtyfold, sixtyfold, even a hundredfold." He added, "If you have ears to hear, then hear" (Mark 4:1-9; see also Matthew 13:1-9, Luke 8:4-8 for parallel versions.)

Biblical Note: The symbol of the sower scattering seed was used occasionally in the ancient world to represent a teacher and the teaching. This parable shows how different hearers respond to the gospel. It is clear that Jesus believed that people could choose to hear and respond.

For Your Meditation: This meditation affirms the past, with its mixed experiences, and the future, with its potential.

Meditation: Take a few deep breaths. Get a sense of yourself on a small hill by a lake. . . . Feel the warmth of the sun. . . . Now, as you look toward the beach, you see people gathered. . . . Notice the Christ standing on a boat, talking to the people. . . . You go down the hill to the shore. . . . As you watch and listen, you hear the Christ talk about seeds which represent how one responds to the gospel. Some seeds fall along footpaths, on the rocky ground, among the thistles, and in good soil. . . . The Christ gives everyone five seeds. . . . Receive your seeds and move away from the crowd, to any place that feels right to sow your seed. . . . Imagine yourself throwing these five seeds, allowing them to land where they will.

The first seed lands upon a footpath. The birds come and eat it up. Allow yourself to reflect upon something in your life that was picked out before it had a full chance to grow. . . . Be aware of your feelings. . . .

The second seed lands upon rocky soil; it takes root, but dies quickly because it has no depth. As you see this seed grow, then die, allow it to represent something in your life that withered because it was not securely rooted. . . . Let yourself feel what occurs. . . .

The third seed lands, grows, but is choked out by thistles. Become aware of something in your life which has been choked out by other interests, activities, values. . . .

Your fourth seed lands, takes root in good soil, grows, and bears fruit. Watch this take place. . . . Now observe what in your life has borne great fruit. Get a sense of that ripe fruit. . . .

Your last seed represents your future. Watch it and allow it to unfold. It may represent an aspect of your life now, as it unfolds in the future, or it may represent something completely new. Allow it to mature. . . . Let the seeds be carried to wherever they want or need to go. . . . Become aware that seeds nurture us and others, far around the world. . . . Sense all these sharings of seeds. Do what you want to do now. Either go back to the hill, finish something with one of the seeds that needs to be finished, or anything else. . . . Become aware of your surroundings, and when you are ready open your eyes.[33]

2. Now write down the five seeds of your imaging then share your experience in this prayer with the group.

3. As a closing prayer the group may use the following corporate intercession. After each *general petition,* such as, "Let us pray for the peace of the world," the leader should allow a time for any person to give a *specific petition,* for example, "especially the conflict in Ireland." After the specific petition has been spoken, the leader continues, "The Lord grant that we may live together in justice and faith." Then the *group response* is, "The Lord hears our prayer."

Leader: Let us pray for the peace of the world.
Specific petition: . . . .
Leader: The Lord grant that we may live together in justice and
  faith.
Group response: The Lord hears our prayer.

Leader: Let us pray for the holy church throughout the world.
Specific petition . . . .
Leader: The Lord keep her unshaken, founded upon the rock of
  his Word, until the end of time.
Group response: The Lord hears our prayer.

Leader: Let us pray for children and young people.
Specific petition: . . . .
Leader: The Lord strengthen them in their vocation.
Group response: The Lord hears our prayer.

Leader: Let us pray for the sick.
Specific petition: . . . .
Leader: The Lord deliver them and restore the strength they
  need.
Group response: The Lord hears our prayer.

Leader: Let us pray for all who are condemned to exile, prison,
  harsh treatment, or hard labor because of their faith in Christ.
Specific petition: . . . .
Leader: The Lord support them and keep them true in faith.
Group response: The Lord hears our prayer.

Leader: Let us remember all the witnesses and martyrs of the
  faith, all who have given their lives for God, and are in
  communion with our brothers and sisters who have fallen
  asleep in Christ.
Specific petition: . . . .
Leader: Let us commit ourselves and one another to the living
  God through Christ our Lord.
Group response: The Lord hears our prayer.[34]

4. Sing a familiar hymn of praise and be dismissed.

The Intercessor 7

DAY ONE
Prays and Lives in the Name

On Days One and Two of Week Five, we considered praying in Jesus' name as a key to effective intercession. Since intercession must grow out of and reflect the life of the intercessor, we need to come back to this matter. It is difficult, in fact, it may be impossible, to pray in Jesus' name unless we live in Jesus' name.

As indicated earlier, the promise of prayer reached its climax in the upper room in Jerusalem. It was a time of revelation and tragedy as Jesus shared that exceedingly memorable time with his disciples—celebrating Passover with his friends—just before his crucifixion. In that setting, the Gospel of John casts some of Jesus' most poignant and powerful words. Here are some of them.

> Whatever you ask in my name, I will do it, that the Father may be glorified in the Son; if you ask anything in my name, I will do it.
> (John 14:13-14, RSV)

> If you abide in me, and my words abide in you, ask whatever you will, and it shall be done for you.
> (John 15:7, RSV).

> You did not choose me, but I chose you and appointed you that you should go and bear fruit and that your fruit should abide; so that whatever you ask the Father in my name, he may give it to you.
> (John 15:16, RSV)

> So you have sorrow now, but I will see you again and your hearts will rejoice, and no one will take your joy from you. In that day you will ask nothing of me. Truly, truly, I say to you, if you ask anything of the Father, he will give it to you in my name. Hitherto you have asked nothing in my name; ask, and you will receive, that your joy may be full.
> I have said this to you in figures; the hour is coming when I shall no longer speak to you in figures but tell you plainly of the Father.
> (John 16:22-25, RSV)

These are extraordinary words stating primarily one extravagant promise: *All things you ask in my name will be granted.* The one condition placed upon this otherwise unconditional promise is "abide in me" and pray "in my name." *The condition required is unity and identity with Christ.*

The intercessor seeks always and primarily to be a person *in Christ.* This means we seek to appropriate the quality of his life. Love and humility, which are expressed in service, reflect this life-quality more distinctively than anything else. Paul describes the Jesus quality of life beautifully.

> Have this mind among yourselves, which you have in Christ Jesus, who, though he was in the form of God, did not count equality with God a thing to be grasped, but emptied himself, taking the form of a servant, being born in the likeness of men. And being found in human form he humbled himself and became obedient unto death, even death on a cross.
>
> (Philippians 2:5-8, RSV)

As intercessors, we seek to have "the mind of Christ," to "abide in him" that our purposes may be one with his.

The extravagant promise of Jesus, then, cannot be seen as something so easy, so free, so mechanical, and rote. "In Jesus' name" is not to be seen as some magical key to unlock any door. In a sense, this formula (if we dare think of it as a formula) is its own safeguard. We can tap the spiritual power offered by Jesus only to the capacity which we develop by living and acting in the name of Jesus. As intercessors, we seek to have "the mind of Christ," to abide in him. Everything depends on our relationship to Christ. The power he has in our life is the power he will express through our prayers. There are other expressions of scripture which help us get perspective on living and praying in that name. *"Do* all in the name of the Lord Jesus" (Colossians 3:17, KJV) is in the same frame of reference as *ask all* "in my name." "We will walk in the name of the Lord" (Micah 4:5, RSV) means that the Lord must rule in the whole of our life.

Prayer, then, emanates from our life, not our lips. When we read scriptural words about "men who have risked their lives for the sake of our Lord Jesus Christ" (Acts 15:26, RSV), or of one "ready not only to be imprisoned but even to die . . . for the name of the Lord Jesus" (Acts 21:13, RSV), we begin to see the requirement of living "in the name." We are then assured that when Christ has everything *of* me, he will obtain everything *for* me. If I let him have everything I have, he will give me everything he has.

REFLECTING AND RECORDING

This is a radical possibility—that when Christ has everything *of* me, he will obtain everything *for* me. If I let him have everything I have, he will give me everything he has. The foundation for the claim is in Jesus' promise, "You must remain united to me and I will remain united to you" (John 15:4, Goodspeed). Also, his word, "Whoever loses his life for my sake will gain it" (Matthew 10:39, TEV).

Spend a few minutes thinking about what that means to you at this point of your Christian commitment and growth.

As a definite act of moving toward a more complete dedication, what is there in your life that you have never yielded to Christ—but would do so now? Record that commitment here.

Christian commitment has been defined as giving as much of myself as I know to as much of Christ as I understand. Pray that as you discover more and more about yourself, you will yield what you discover to Christ.

DURING THE DAY

Take this thought with you today: When I have yielded as much of myself as I know to as much of Christ as I understand, I am totally committed and Jesus is Lord of my life.

DAY TWO
Mary and Martha: Getting the Story Straight

> Now as they went on their way, he entered a village; and a woman named Martha received him into her house. And she had a sister called Mary, who sat at the Lord's feet and listened to his teaching. But Martha was distracted with much serving; and she went to him and said, "Lord, do you not care that my sister has left me to serve alone? Tell her then to help me." But the Lord answered her, "Martha, Martha, you are anxious and troubled about many things; one thing is needful. Mary has chosen the good portion, which shall not be taken away from her."
>
> (Luke 10:38-42, RSV)

Poor Martha! She has been the brunt of so many sermons, lambasted for her attention to work and her irritation at Mary for not helping her. How often is this story used as an illustration of the attention we should give to spiritual rather than material things!

Not for the sake of Martha but for our own sakes let's get the story straight. It is not a dichotomy of spiritual and material. It is not mysticism versus realism. The spiritual interest of Mary is not set against the work of Martha. *The attention Mary gives to the presence of Jesus as opposed to*

Martha's agitation and preoccupation with tasks—this is the focus of the teaching. Martha's work is not oriented and ordered by the presence of Jesus.

There are two possible dangers as we seek to find meaning for ourselves in this incident. The stance of Mary, her choosing "the better part," has been set against the action of Martha. Though probably not as common in our day as in previous generations, there is an exalting of the place of prayer and a diminishing of the importance of action. This is the first danger. This interpretation was present to a marked degree in the monastic movements of the church—removing oneself from the world of action and involvement, choosing the "better way" of prayer, meditation, reflection. There is a sense in which this reduces this world to an inferior status—a kind of waiting room for the Kingdom.

When taken to its extreme, as it has often been, this stance of exalting the importance of prayer and diminishing the importance of action contradicts the meaning of the Incarnation. It also makes prayer much less than that conscious attitude of presence and attention before God which is to pervade the whole of life in order that we may be extensions of the Incarnation; that is, that we may be Christ's presence in the world.

But there is a second danger that may be more pervasive in our time. This danger is expressed in the affirmation: "My life and action are my prayer."

There is a bit of truth in the statement. It disallows a dichotomy in the Christian life, refusing to separate prayer and action. But the danger in the stance is greater than what it seeks to combat. One possible danger is that we might simply use such an affirmation as an excuse for not being more spiritually disciplined. The greater danger is that earnest persons may become so absorbed with great causes—justice, peace, etc.—so involved in action that they will lose sight of *the presence of Christ,* "the one thing needful."

My life and action should be my prayer. But there is a possible illusion here. It is essential that we make the whole of our lives a presence before God. But to assume our lives already are a presence before him may be naive, even pretentious and presumptuous. The question is, how can there be a conscious waiting for God, an intentional presence before him, without taking a specific form and involving a particular discipline of time and attention?

The problem Jesus addresses with Martha is not that of *busyness* but *fragmentation.* Jesus did not chide Martha for attending to many things rather than one, but for being troubled or frustrated by it all. It is not *quiet* so much as *wholeness* we are to seek. God awaits us not only in solitude, but in our friendships, in our involvements and actions.

So, we *presence* ourselves in set times of prayer, deliberately, intentionally. A part of this "presencing" is our intercession. We bring our concerns to Christ, we present them in love to him, we call for his intervention, and we offer ourselves to be the answer for which we pray.

On Day Four of Week Two, I shared the story of my wife Jerry praying for Kay. Jerry is an artist. As a result of her praying, she began to produce a story for little Kay. She illustrated it with some of the most beautiful drawings and watercolors she has ever done. Each week, for about ten weeks, she sent Kay additions to the story—a story about a little girl named

"Kay" who played with imaginary characters down by the creek behind our house. It was a beautiful story, and some of Jerry's finest art.

We never heard from Kay, but perhaps her last weeks were made more bearable, perhaps even cheerful, because of those weekly "visits" from someone who first began to pray.

REFLECTING AND RECORDING

We are often called to *be our intercession.* We pray for the hungry. God responds, "I will answer your prayer. What will you do for the hungry?" We pray for the lonely, and again God says, "I hear you. What will you be for the lonely?" We pray for peace in the world and God answers, "Peace is my dream and peace begins with you. How will you be a peacemaker?"

Let this guide your reflection. "Presence" yourself with the Lord; bring your concerns to him, and see what happens in a specific time of prayer before you proceed with the other activities of the day.

DURING THE DAY

Be in intercession throughout the day as you have been specifically guided in this period, and/or as you will be guided throughout the day.

DAY THREE
The World's Sin Is Our Own

> The law of the Lord is perfect,
>   reviving the soul;
> the testimony of the Lord is sure,
>   making wise the simple;
> the precepts of the Lord are right,
>   rejoicing the heart;
> the commandment of the Lord is pure,
>   enlightening the eyes;
> the fear of the Lord is clean,
>   enduring for ever;
> the ordinances of the Lord are true,
>   and righteous altogether.
> More to be desired are they than gold,
>   even much fine gold;
> sweeter also than honey
>   and drippings of the honeycomb.

Moreover by them is thy servant warned;
  in keeping them there is great reward.
But who can discern his errors?
  Clear thou me from hidden faults.
Keep back thy servant also from presumptuous sins;
  let them not have dominion over me!
Then I shall be blameless,
  and innocent of great transgression.

Let the words of my mouth and the meditation of my heart
  be acceptable in thy sight,
  O Lord, my rock and my redeemer.
  (Psalm 19:7-18, RSV)

In our praying we come inevitably to pray for the forgiveness of our sin—especially particular sins which are glaringly obvious to us. The psalmist was aware that it is often difficult to discuss our errors, and that we needed to be cleared of hidden faults and kept back from presumtuous sins. The sin of our life is to be reflected upon, and we are to keep constant vigilance against thinking that we are without sin.

As intercessors, we also pray for the sins of others, that particular persons about whom we are concerned may accept God's gracious forgiveness and experience freedom from guilt and find newness of life.

There is a dramatic word in First John which brings to focus the work of Christ in relation to sin: "My little children, I am writing this to you so that you may not sin; but if any one does sin, we have an advocate with the Father, Jesus Christ the righteous; and he is the expiation for our sins, and not for ours only but also for the sins of the whole world" (1 John 2:1-2, RSV).

In our praying we are driven to recognize that it is not our sin alone, or the sins of our loved ones and friends about which we are to be concerned, "but also for the sins of the whole world." This concern shapes the life of the intercessor. Penitence for our own sin calls us to be penitent and to intercede for the sins of the whole world.

It is no sentimental theory which asserts that all persons have responsibility towards the common and corporate sin of humankind. *The world's sin is our own sin.* George S. Stewart reminds us of that.

We cannot passively acquiesce or treat it as inevitable. We share responsibility for it, and when we face that till it wounds and pains, then we are taking our proper place in the brotherhood of mankind. The misery and weariness of the world's sin becomes part of our own pain, so that the heart is filled with pity and with purpose to seek, that saving grace be brought into contact with the sin of the world. Here, too, hopefulness and expectation are born. The sin of others is united with our penitence and with our experience of the loving-kindness and the saving mercies of Christ. We bring men penitence by repenting. We learn to hope for the world, because we have found boundless mercy towards ourselves and cannot despair for others. So penitence is bound up with intercession as with thanksgiving.[35]

REFLECTING AND RECORDING

7

Look at the city or community in which you live. What are the sins as you perceive them? List here in sentences or words.

Reflect upon these questions and jot down some of your thoughts. In what way do I share responsibility for the sins of my city or community?

In what way do these sins affect my life? The life of my family?

What would I designate as the corporate sins of the world?

In what way do I share responsibility for these sins? (This may require deep probing, but probe.)

In what way do these sins affect my life? The life of my family?

Make the following prayer of Michel Quoist your own.

Lord, . . .
I ask forgiveness for all those who sleep, or who are so paralysed, frustrated, self-
centered, indifferent, discouraged and disgusted
    that they no longer try to grow,
    that they no longer know how to grow,
    that they no longer want to grow,
and who therefore put down their arms and withdraw,
    leaving their brothers to fight alone.
Above all, Lord, I ask your forgiveness for myself.
I've passed by these wounded, captive ones
    without seeing them,
    or without going to them: "He saw him, and continued on his way."
I did not offer them the opportunity
    to awaken,
    to begin to live again,
    to rejoin their brothers in battle.
Lord, let me sit each day at the side of the well,
    tired, perhaps, but still alert.
Let me be the one who asks passers-by,
    for myself and my brothers:
    "Give me a drink."
Forgive us, Lord, for "there are too many people whom we just leave asleep." [36]

DURING THE DAY

Be especially sensitive to what you see around you today, what you see on television or read in the newspaper that you would call "sin." Make these "sins" *your own* as you bring them to God with your own repentant spirit.

DAY FOUR
The World's Suffering Must Be Our Own

Not only is the world's sin our own, the world's suffering must be our own. On Day Four of Week Five, we considered brokenness of spirit as a channel through which God moves to minister to others. "The sacrifice acceptable to God is a broken spirit" (Psalm 51:17, RSV).

Sin and suffering are intimately connected. I do not mean that all suffering is a result of sin. My physical illness or emotional trauma certainly may not be a result of my sin. Always to seek a cause/effect relationship between sin and suffering in individuals is unfair to say the least, and often devastating emotionally and spiritually.

7

With that perspective, however, we must affirm that there is often a connection between sin and suffering. The good news is that Christ is Lord of life and death, and he offers liberating power for sin and suffering. Over and over again, in a rich variety of cases, the parables and miracles of Jesus become signs of this liberating power.

Mark's story of the healing of the paralytic presents an interesting sequence of liberation. Four men broke through the roof of the house where Jesus was teaching because they found no other way to bring their paralytic friend into Jesus' presence. When Jesus saw their faith, he said to the fellow who was sick of palsy, "Son, thy sins be forgiven thee." Then came the rub.

> "Why does this man speak thus? It is blasphemy! Who can forgive sins but God alone?" And immediately Jesus, perceiving in his spirit that they thus questioned within themselves, said to them, "Why do you question thus in your hearts? Which is easier, to say to the paralytic, 'Your sins are forgiven,' or to say, 'Rise, take up your pallet and walk'? But that you may know that the Son of man has authority on earth to forgive sins"—he said to the paralytic—"I say to you, rise, take up your pallet and go home."
>
> (Mark 2:7-12, RSV)

Here the ministry of Jesus is focused: *forgiveness* and *healing.*

The Christian's response to sickness and suffering is not resignation. We are not to submit passively to pain and suffering any more than to sin. Confession of sin, vigilance against it, and pardon for it are in close relation to healing. The Epistle of James admonishes, "Confess your sins to one another, and pray for one another, that you may be healed" (James 5:16, RSV).

Being raised with Christ to newness of life means inner freedom and bodily wholeness which come through forgiveness and healing.

The intercessor, accepting and experiencing the liberating power of Jesus over sin and suffering, joins his adoration and thanksgiving to God for his own deliverance with intercession for all those who suffer. This is a difficult work. Somehow—and who can tell us how?—our task is to cultivate awareness and become so sensitive to the suffering of others that in prayer, and to the degree possible, in our action, we take upon ourselves their suffering.

Prayer, especially intercession, is an expression of our greatest love. Instead of keeping pain away from us, loving prayer leads us into the suffering of God and of others. The deeper our love of God, the deeper our love of others. The deeper our love, the more we will suffer. The more we suffer, the more we will pray.

Our suffering and the suffering of others is embraced by the compassionate Christ. In a way that we may never fully understand, our intercession, through identity with suffering, becomes a channel of Christ's liberating power.

REFLECTING AND RECORDING

Think of persons you know who are suffering:

Name a person here who is suffering physically.

_____

Name one who is experiencing emotional anguish.

_____

Name one who is suffering the pain of loss through the death of a loved one.

_____

Name one who is experiencing depression and despair for some reason you may not even know.

_____

One after another, hold each of the persons you have named in your heart. Get a picture of them clearly in your mind. Try to feel their pain, their anguish, their lifelessness. Stay with your feelings with and for them until you get at least a hint of what they are experiencing. Now as an act of love and surrender to God, offer to him in a prayer what you feel. Receive his love on behalf of the one with whom you are identifying, and visualize that person receiving God's love and peace and strength.

Repeat your prayer of identification with each person you named above.

As you sense your inability to fully enter the pain of others, offer that feeling to God. Ask that you may be more sensitive and learn to translate your concern into a willingness to make the suffering of others your own. It is the *willingness* that counts.

DURING THE DAY

What can you do for one or two of the persons named above to let them know you care? Decide now. Write what you decide here.

Make an intentional decision to follow through today.

7

DAY FIVE
God Speaks to Our Wounds and Through Our Wounds

A modern poet has expressed the thought that where we are wounded—it is there that God speaks to us. We do not have to believe that God sends our wounds, that he is responsible for our suffering. I don't. I do believe, because I have experienced it and know numerous others who have also, that it is in the depths of suffering that we are most open to what God has to say to us. In Jesus' allegory of the vine and branches (John 15) it is clear that we must endure pruning in order to bear fruit.

God speaks to our wounds and through our wounds.

Consider Paul's witness.

> And to keep me from being too elated by the abundance of revelations, a thorn was given me in the flesh, a messenger of Satan, to harass me, to keep me from being too elated. Three times I besought the Lord about this, that it should leave me; but he said to me, "My grace is sufficient for you, for my power is made perfect in weakness." I will all the more gladly boast of my weakness, that the power of Christ may rest upon me. For the sake of Christ, then, I am content with weaknesses, insults, hardships, persecutions, and calamities, for when I am weak, then I am strong.
>
> (1 Cor. 12:7-10, RSV)

There is mystery in pain. We should not hesitate to affirm that God wills physical as well as spiritual wholeness. As we saw yesterday, there is a close relation between the two.

Yet, Christians are often sick. Christians know pain and infirmity—even physical limitation and deformity from which they are not delivered. Paul's classic "thorn in the flesh" is not foreign to most of us, for we have our thorns.

Paul shares his experience of suffering in a very interesting context. He has referred to visions and revelations that have been his, unspeakable words he has heard, and the glorious paradise he has experienced. Yet, he does not tell us what these mysterious revelations and visions were, only that Christ has honored him with them.

Then he tells of the "thorn in the flesh" but gives no details about it either. So, the ecstasy and the agony remain shrouded in mystery.

There has been a lot of speculation about what this thorn of Paul's was. We don't need to reiterate those speculations. I believe it is providential that Paul did not tell us what it was. His contemporaries may have known, but we remain ignorant that we may understand our situation is in principle the same as Paul's. We have our thorn, and what Paul says about his instructs us in our pilgrimage.

The lesson is clear for me. The goal of our praying is not primarily for deliverance from pain and suffering, but that God's will shall be done, that God's purposes shall be accomplished, that Christ's sufficient grace shall be realized.

REFLECTING AND RECORDING

We will consider this more tomorrow. For now, reflect on your own wounds.

What would you designate as your "thorn in the flesh" from which you have not been delivered? Record here.

Reflect upon your "thorn" and write a few sentences describing what has happened in your life as a result of this thorn. Be honest, putting into words thoughts you may not have recorded before.

DURING THE DAY

Yesterday you were asked to express your care for some person who is suffering. If you were not able to follow through, do so today. If you were able to do so, select another or two for specific expressions of your concern today. Name them here, and write what your action will be in relation to them.

DAY SIX
Count It All Joy

7

There is a fascinating and challenging word in the first chapter of James.

> Count it all joy, my brethren, when you meet various trials, for you know that the testing of your faith produces steadfastness. And let steadfastness have its full effect, that you may be perfect and complete, lacking in nothing.
>
> If any of you lacks wisdom, let him ask God, who gives to all men generously and without reproaching, and it will be given him.
>
> But let him ask in faith, with no doubting, for he who doubts is like a wave of the sea that is driven and tossed by the wind. For that person must not suppose that a double-minded man, unstable in all his ways, will receive anything from the Lord.
>
> (James 1:2-8, RSV)

There are four significant lessons here for the intercessor:

1. If we lack wisdom, God will give it (verse 5).

2. We must ask in faith, not doubting (verse 6).

3. We must be single-minded, (verses 7-8), intent on God's will and purpose, living and praying in the name of Christ.

4. The fourth lesson is a continuation of our reflection yesterday. "Count it all joy, . . . when you meet various trials." This is the mystery of pain—God's speaking to and through our wounds—molding our character, building our faith, cultivating our sensitivity, breaking our spirits until we become channels through which his healing, sustaining, transforming love can flow.

I remember vividly when this lesson came clearly to me. I referred earlier to a serious auto accident which left me with a broken leg, broken ribs, and a punctured lung. It was a time of trauma, physically, mentally, and spiritually. Yet it became a "count it all joy" experience. I write a lot during my prayer period. One day, while still recuperating, I wrote the following:

> Lord, it seems as though you've decided
>   to keep vivid signs from me.
> I suppose you know how gullible and
>   fickle I am.
> Seeing is always believing for me.
>   Maybe you know I don't always see clearly,
>   and signs are often misread by me.
> So, I've quit putting out fleeces,
>   and I just struggle to believe.
>   I keep on waiting and trusting
>   and longing.
> Well, Lord, thank you.
>   Thank you big!
> You've confirmed my waiting and trusting
>   and longing,
>   not with a sign
>   but with your presence,
>   your vivid presence,
> You have "tented" with me
>   for days.

The nightmare of a head-on collision
  broken leg, broken ribs, pierced lung
  has been transformed into an incredible
  experience of peace and quietness and
  confidence and knowing.
The miracle has been my consciousness of
  your healing presence.
What a miracle that is.
I'd like to build a tabernacle here on
  Mt. Tabor, Lord,
  even with this clumsy leg cast and
  aching muscles and painful breathing.
But I remember some others who wanted to stay on
  Mt. Tabor.
  You wouldn't let them,
  and you won't let me.
You even took them to Gethsemane.
  How different from Mt. Tabor.
I know that when we build permanent temples
  where you have been with us in
  temporary tents,
  we don't "house" you.
  We only box ourselves in.
  I won't do that.
  But I won't forget our "tenting" together.
  And when my insatiable longing for a
    sign wells up again,
I'll fight the temptation to put out
  a fleece.
And will remember our Mt. Tabor.

It is an obvious truth, but so often overlooked. *It is not the power of prayer, but the power of the living Lord, which comes through prayer, that we seek.* Therefore we don't struggle *with* prayer, we struggle *in* prayer. We struggle against evil and suffering, against our own selfishness and greed, against our "why me, Lord" syndrome. It is as we struggle in prayer that we are able to "count it all joy" because we make the meaningful discovery that God not only speaks *to* our wounds, but also *through* our wounds.

God often speaks *to* our wounds saying, "My grace is sufficient." Paul affirmed that God refused to deliver him from his thorn to keep him from being elated. Can we see our wounds as a dynamic power operating to keep us humble?

Paul saw his thorn as a "messenger of Satan to harass" him. But he turned that harassment into glory for God. God can speak *through* our wounds enabling us to identify with others, to speak to them in their pain. God can speak through our pain to purify us, to make us patient, to sensitize us to the feelings of others, to unite us with others that we might lift their suffering to Christ in our deepest intercession.

REFLECTING AND RECORDING

Look back at what you wrote yesterday. Reflect upon whether your thorn has been a "messenger of Satan to harrass" you or an instrument of God.

God's answer to Paul's prayer for deliverance from his "thorn in the flesh" was, "My grace is sufficient." Can you accept that as God's possible answer to you and give him your "thorn" as an instrument of his glory? Do so by writing a prayer of commitment.

DURING THE DAY

Paul said the word he received from God was, "My grace is sufficient for you, for my power is made perfect in weakness." God always answers our prayer. Either he changes the circumstances or he supplies sufficient power to overcome them. This affirmation is printed on page 155. Clip it and carry it with you in the days ahead as an empowering conviction.

Maybe you would like to call or write someone you know who needs this affirmation today.

DAY SEVEN
Intercession Through Identity

It is easy for us to forget—in fact, never to consider—that Jesus experienced failure. In our emphasis upon the love and power we receive from him and the limitless promises he offers to those who live and pray in his name, we pass over the fact that his ministry was fragile, somewhat fragmentary. The all-inclusiveness of his humanity is crucial to our understanding of his life and prayer. And certainly crucial to our experience of prayer.

> For we have not a high priest who is unable to sympathize with our weaknesses,
> but one who in every respect has been tempted as we are, yet without sinning. Let
> us then with confidence draw near to the throne of grace, that we may receive
> mercy and find grace to help in time of need.
> (Hebrews 4:15-16, RSV)

The more we seek to pray in the name and spirit of Jesus, the more we are driven to experience our own weakness and finitude. We remember Gethsemane and the anguish of Jesus as he embraced his own finitude. The writer to the Hebrews makes the case that Jesus' suffering and temptation prepared him to be our priest, our great intercessor. "For because he himself has suffered and been tempted, he is able to help those who are tempted" (Hebrews 2:18, RSV).

> So Jesus also suffered outside the gate in order to sanctify the people through his own blood. Therefore let us go forth to him outside the camp, bearing abuse for him. For here we have no lasting city, but we seek the city which is to come. Through him then let us continually offer up a sacrifice of praise to God, that is, the fruit of lips that acknowledge his name. Do not neglect to do good and to share what you have, for such sacrifices are pleasing to God.
> (Hebrews 13:12-16, RSV)

As intercessors, we are to embrace our own weakness and finitude, and the weakness and finitude of others. How do we pray for all the poor, the hungry who are dying for lack of food with every tick of the clock? How do we pray for a world that is rushing headlong into self-destruction by its intent upon nuclear proliferation? How do we pray for the reign of peace in a world so torn apart by national pride, selfish ideology, and opposing values?

We intercede by identification. We seek to live in solidarity with the poor, the oppressed, the suffering of the world. Sometimes we can do that literally, physically—enter into the darkness of the sufferer. But most of the time we can't. So our praying becomes a profession of faith. We position ourselves before the God of justice, mercy, and righteousness. We stand with our brother, the suffering Christ. Knowing that in his earthly sojourn of full humanity, Jesus did not meet every need, we anguish with him, as he anguished over Jerusalem. Feel the pain in his heart as he cries out in these words recorded in Matthew 23:37 (RSV): "Jerusalem, Jerusalem, killing the prophets and stoning those who are sent to you! How often would I have gathered your children together as a hen gathers her brood under her wings, and you would not!"

Our intercession becomes identification, and our praying is like that described by Paul. "Likewise the Spirit helps us in our weakness; for we do not know how to pray as we ought, but the Spirit himself intercedes for us with sighs too deep for words. And he who searches the hearts of men knows what is the mind of the Spirit, because the Spirit intercedes for the saints according to the will of God" (Romans 8:26-27, RSV).

We live in hope that our identification with Jesus in his anguish for the whole of creation is not wasted. Nay, more! Not the *is now* but the *will be* is the basis for our hope. Jesus was *anticipation of kingdom*. The gift of his Spirit is the *earnest* (guarantee) of what is to come.

"In him you also, who have heard the word of truth, the gospel of your salvation, and have believed in him, were sealed with the promised Holy Spirit, which is the guarantee of our inheritance until we acquire possession of it, to the praise of his glory" (Ephesians 1:13-14, RSV).

7

REFLECTING AND RECORDING

Spend as much time as you can reflecting upon your experience during these weeks you have been using the workbook. What insights have come? What feelings? What are your reservations and doubts? What commitments have you made or will you make? As your thoughts and feelings come, write them here.

Your workbook experience is finished. How do you intend to proceed in a disciplined life of prayer? Are there specific decisions and commitments you have made or will make to intercession? Record here.

DURING THE DAY AND ALL DAYS TO COME

Move in relation to others, knowing that we are linked with one another and with God; that God uses us and our prayers as the channels of his grace, love, and power.

If you are in a group, you will meet sometime today. Plan to make that meeting a joyful celebration as you share your reflections written above. Think particularly of persons in the group who have been especially meaningful to you. Don't fail to express your gratitude.

GROUP MEETING FOR WEEK SEVEN

INTRODUCTION

The dynamic rhythm of reflection and action are the essential elements in the pattern of living prayer. The contemplative life is really a life that is rooted in reflection upon God's will and way, and is acted out in faithfulness and obedience to him. This calls for discipline—intentionally being alone with God, reflecting upon how God comes to us, seeking God's will, appropriating God's strength, and acting according to the guidance we have. We seek to live his life in the world by checking our signals with him and other Christian pilgrims.

If you are not continuing this group experience, explore the possibility of forming a covenant with one or two persons in a continuing ministry of intercession. There is great strength in being united with a few people in intercessory concern—staying in touch by phone or in person, sharing concerns about which you are mutually praying.*

If some wish to continue the group, spend some time (perhaps at the close of the meeting) determining your content and format for study, making your plans, deciding schedules and meeting places.

SHARING TOGETHER

1. Let persons share their most meaningful day and most difficult day with the workbook this week.

2. Let each person express in two or three sentences only the most significant discovery each one has made about prayer in this seven-week intercessory prayer experience.

3. Now ask participants to look at the notes they wrote in their reflection time today. Spend thirty minutes or so in the group talking about the insights which have come during this seven weeks—the feelings, the reservations, the doubts, the joys. Persons may want to expand on what they shared as the most significant discovery they have made in their intercessory prayer experience.

4. Give an opportunity for persons to share whatever decision or commitment they have made, or will make, to an ongoing life of intercession.

PRAYING TOGETHER

1. Begin your time of prayer by asking each person to express gratitude to God in a two- or three-sentence prayer for something significant that has happened to him/her as a result of these seven weeks.

2. Continue with corporate prayers of gratitude in the form of each person sharing one answer to intercessory prayer experienced during these seven weeks. After the sharing by each person, the entire group responds, *"We thank you, Lord Jesus."*

3. Since this may be the last meeting, some persons in the group may have special concerns or personal needs for which they wish the group to pray. Some may wish the entire group to lay hands upon them as they pray. Give this opportunity.

---

* The Upper Room has a network of *Covenant Groups* throughout the nation who are linked in intercession. For information write 1908 Grand Avenue, Nashville, Tennessee 37202.

4. A benediction is a blessing or greeting shared with another or by a group in parting. The "passing of the peace" is such a benediction. You take a person's hands, look into his/her eyes and say, "The peace of God be with you," and the person responds, "And may God's peace be yours." Then that person, taking the hands of the person next to him or her, says "The peace of God be yours," and receives the response, "And may God's peace be yours." Standing in a circle, let the leader "pass the peace," and let it go around the circle.

5. Having completed the passing of the peace, then, in closing, greet one another in a more spontaneous way. Move about to different persons in the group, saying and doing whatever you feel is appropriate for your parting blessing to each person. You may shake hands and say, "May you always be sensitive to the blessing of God's presence with you." Or, you may hold both hands of the person, look him/her in the eyes saying, "I love you and I know God loves you." Or, you may simply embrace the person and say nothing. In your own unique way, "bless" each person who has shared this journey with you.

Notes

1. Frank C. Laubach, *Prayer* (Westwood, N.J.: Fleming H. Revell Co., 1946), pp. 21-22.

2. *Ibid.*, p. 22.

3. Harry Emerson Fosdick, *The Meaning of Prayer* (New York: Association Press, 1962), pp. 29-30.

4. Andrew Murray, *The Ministry of Intercession* (New York: Fleming H. Revell Co., 1898), p. 139.

5. James Carroll, *Tender of Wishes* (New York: Newman Press, 1969), p. 136.

6. Alexander Whyte, *Lord, Teach Us to Pray* (London: Hodder and Stoughton, 1922), pp. 170-71.

7. Pierre-Yves Emery, *Prayer at the Heart of Life* (Maryknoll, N.Y.: Orbis Books, 1975), pp. 6-8.

8. Henry Bett, *The Reality of the Religious Life* (New York: Macmillan, 1949), p. 61.

9. C. S. Lewis, *The Screwtape Letters* (New York: Macmillan, 1943), p. 137.

10. Rufus Jones, *Pathway to the Reality of God* (New York: Macmillan, 1931), p. 253.

11. Pierre-Yves Emery, *Prayer at the Heart of Life* (Maryknoll, N. Y.: Orbis Books, 1975), pp. 132-133.

12. *Ibid.,* p. 133.

13. Huub Oosterhuis, *Your Word Is Near* (New York: Paulist Press, 1968), pp. 13-14.

14. Pierre-Yves Emery, *Prayer at the Heart of Life* (Maryknoll, N. Y.: Orbis Books, 1975), pp. 136-137.

15. Walter Rauschenbusch, *Prayers of the Social Awakening* (Boston: The Pilgrim Press, 1909), pp. 123-24.

16. John Baillie, *Christian Devotion* (London: Oxford University Press, 1962), p. 26.

17. Clarence McConkey, *A Burden and an Ache* (Nashville: Abingdon, 1970), pp. 28-29.

18. Lewis Maclachlan, *The Teaching of Jesus on Prayer* (London: James Clarke & Co., Ltd., 1952), p. 49.

19. Jack W. Hayford, *Prayer Is Invading the Impossible* (Plainfield, N. J.: Logos International, 1977), p. 66.

20. Lewis Maclachlan, *The Teaching of Jesus on Prayer* (London: The Camelot Press, Ltd., 1952), p. 50.

21. Harry Emerson Fosdick, *The Meaning of Prayer* (New York: Association Press, 1962), p. 173.

22. *Ibid.,* pp. 184-85.

23. *Ibid.,* p. 179.

24. Jo Kimmel, *Steps to Prayer Power* (Nashville: Abingdon Press, 1972), p. 12.

25. Leslie Brandt, *God Is Here—Let's Celebrate* (St. Louis: Concordia Publishing House, 1970). pp. 22-23.

26. Carolyn Stahl, *Opening to God* (Nashville: The Upper Room, 1977), pp. 63-64.

27. L. Robert Keck, *The Spirit of Synergy: God's Power and You* (Nashville: Abingdon, 1978), p. 126.

28. Russell Targ, in *The Spirit of Synergy: God's Power and You* (Nashville: Abingdon Press, 1978), p. 139.

29. Allan A. Hunter, *Preventive Prayer and Meditation* (Ashland, Ohio: Disciplined Order of Christ), p. 4.

30. Leslie Brandt, *God Is Here—Let's Celebrate* (St. Louis: Concordia, 1970), pp. 22-23.

31. *Ibid.,* pp. 19-20.

32. Jo Kimmel, *Steps to Prayer Power* (Nashville: Abingdon, 1972), pp. 29, 34-35.

33. Carolyn Stahl, *Opening to God* (Nashville: The Upper Room, 1977), pp. 59-60.

34. Adapted from *Praise in All Our Days, Common Prayer at Taizé,* tr. by Emily Chisholm (Leighton Buzzard, Beds., Great Britain, The Faith Press, English translation 1975), pp. 240-41.

35. George S. Stewart, *The Lower Levels of Prayer* (Edinburgh: The Saint Andrew Press, Revised Ed., copyright Alison Stewart, 1969), pp. 79-80.

36. Michael Quoist, *Meet Christ and Live* (Dublin, Ireland: Gill and Macmillan, 1973), pp. 80-81. © by Michael Quoist, 1972; translation © Doubleday & Company, Inc. 1973.

Appendix

CLIP 3

My God hears me— and answers!

My God hears me— and answers!

CLIP 2

CLIP 1

But now thus says the Lord,
  he who created you, _____,
  he who formed you, _____:
"Fear not, for I have redeemed you;
  I have called you by name, you are
mine.
When you pass through the waters
   I will be with you, _____;
  and through the rivers, they shall
   not overwhelm you;
when you walk through fire you,
    _____, shall not be burned,
  and the flame shall not consume you.
For I am the Lord your God,
  The Holy One of Israel, your Savior."
                (Isaiah 43:1-3a, RSV)

"Ask, and it will be given you;
seek, and you will find; knock,
and it will be opened to you.
For every one who seeks receives,
and he who seeks finds, and to
him who knocks it will be opened.
Or what man of you, if his son
asks him for bread, will give
him a stone? Or if he asks for
a fish, will give him a serpent?
If you then, who are evil, know
how to give good gifts to your
children, how much more will your
Father who is in heaven give good
things to those who ask him!"
           (Matt. 7:7-11, RSV)

But now thus says the Lord,
  he who created you, _____,
  he who formed you, _____:
"Fear not, for I have redeemed you;
  I have called you by name, you are
mine.
When you pass through the waters
   I will be with you, _____;
  and through the rivers, they shall
   not overwhelm you;
when you walk through fire you,
   _____, shall not be burned,
  and the flame shall not consume you.
For I am the Lord your God,
  The Holy One of Israel, your Savior."
                 (Isaiah 43:1-3a, RSV)

CLIP 4

But now thus says the Lord,
  he who created you, _____,
  he who formed you, _____:
"Fear not, for I have redeemed you;
  I have called you by name, you are
mine.
When you pass through the waters
   I will be with you, _____;
  and through the rivers, they shall
   not overwhelm you;
when you walk through fire you,
   _____, shall not be burned,
  and the flame shall not consume you.
For I am the Lord your God,
  The Holy One of Israel, your Savior."
                 (Isaiah 43:1-3a, RSV)

CLIP 4

But now thus says the Lord,
  he who created you, _____,
  he who formed you, _____:
"Fear not, for I have redeemed you;
  I have called you by name, you are
mine.
When you pass through the waters
   I will be with you, _____;
  and through the rivers, they shall
   not overwhelm you;
when you walk through fire you,
   _____, shall not be burned,
  and the flame shall not consume you.
For I am the Lord your God,
  The Holy One of Israel, your Savior."
                 (Isaiah 43:1-3a, RSV)

Prayer List

ONGOING   **IMMEDIATE**

CLIP 9

My grace is sufficient for you, for my power is made perfect in weakness. —2 Cor. 12:9, RSV

God always answers our prayer Either he changes the circumstances, or he supplies sufficient power to overcome them.

CLIP 8

URGENT LIST

CLIP 7

The Lord is near; have no anxiety, but in everything make your requests known to God in prayer and petition with thanksgiving. Then the peace of God, which is beyond our utmost understanding, will keep guard over your hearts and your thoughts, in Christ Jesus.
  —Phil. 4:6-7, NEB

CLIP 6

For with thee is the fountain of life; in thy light do we see light. —Ps. 36:9, RSV